D0411049
花馬龍紙折
花馬龍紙折
花馬龍紙折
花馬龍紙折
花馬龍紙折
花馬龍紙折

The Art of ORIGAMI

STEVE and MEGUMI BIDDLE

Published and distributed by
TOBAR LIMITED
St. Margaret, Harleston, Norfolk, IP20 0TB, UK
www.tobar.co.uk

First edition published in Great Britain in 2003
by Connections Book Publishing Limited
This edition published in Great Britain in 2004

British Library Cataloguing-in-Publication data available on request.

ISBN 1-903230-14-4

10 9 8 7 6 5 4 3 2

Phototypeset in Amazone BT, Stone and Folio using QuarkXPress on Apple Macintosh
Origination by Bright Arts, Singapore
Printed by Hung Hing Offset Printing Co. Ltd, China

Contents

Foreword

Welcome to the fabulous world of origami, the art of paper folding. Origami can be enjoyed by anybody, regardless of age, nationality or language. Each year more and more people are joining the growing numbers of enthusiasts exploring the pleasures of origami.

There is more to origami than just folding paper; there is magic in transforming a flat square of paper into a three-dimensional piece of art, breathing life into an otherwise static object. The very act of folding stimulates and enriches the imagination, creating ideas and improving hand and eye coordination. Such focus calls for a Zen-like concentration, a meditation that can also create an enormous sense of calm and relaxation. For when our attention is fully engaged, the mind becomes silent; when we succeed in restricting our thoughts to one subject, the incessant internal chattering stops. Indeed, the contentment we feel when our minds are absorbed often comes less from the activity itself, than from the fact that in concentrating, our worries or problems are forgotten.

Origami promotes the joy of giving and receiving. A paper sculpture is created and given to a friend as a gift (the way it is presented can say a lot about the care and thought that went into its creation). The friend learns the skill and makes another model, and so the craft, the desire to learn and share, and the gesture of friendship are all perpetuated.

Steve and Megumi Biddle

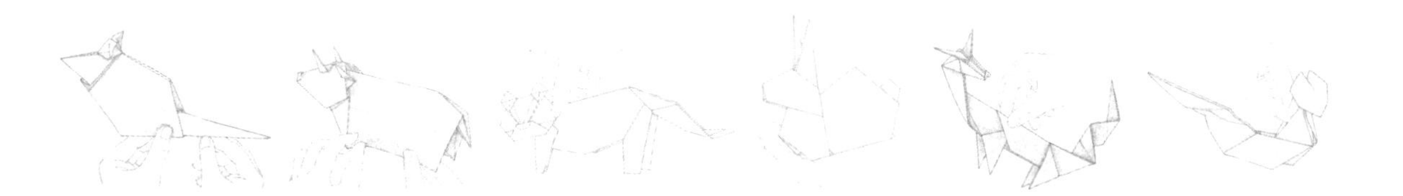

The Origins of Origami

The ancient Chinese were the inventors of paper, its origin being attributed to Tsai Lun, in the year 105 CE. *The main tradition of paper folding in China was discovered within the Chinese tradition of funerary art, in which replicas or representations of money or household goods are tossed onto coffins as symbols of objects for the departed to take with them into the next world.*

For more than five hundred years, the Chinese kept the art of making paper a secret. Then in the eighth century, Chinese invaders who were captured in Arabia were forced to reveal the technique. Eventually the process reached southern Europe. The Spanish symbol of paper folding – the *pajarita,* or 'little bird' – is said to have existed in the seventeenth century. Elsewhere in Europe, paper folding took place in the form of decorative napkin folds. Paper-making methods were introduced into Japan (from China, by way of Korea) with the spread of Buddhism during the Asuka era (593–686). The missionaries used paper for the inscription of *sutras* – Buddhist prayers – and so spread, not only 'the word', but also the medium upon which it was written. It is also interesting to note that the Japanese word *kami* can mean 'God', as well as 'paper'. The two meanings are distinguished by the characters, which are written differently. This has given rise to a belief that paper is sacred. It has long been associated with the Shinto religion and the folding of *hitogata* – human figures – that are blessed by God.

Origami in everyday life

Origami wasn't practised for personal enjoyment during ancient times, because paper was scarce and therefore very valuable. It probably became a little more widespread during the Heian period (794–1185), with the development of elaborate ceremonial and recreational paper folds. During the Muromachi period (1333–1568), origami styles served to distinguish the aristocratic samurai from the lower-class farmers and peasants. As this period was one of military rule, people knew their place in society, and therefore they folded accordingly. It was during the Edo period (1600–1868), a time of development in

the arts, that paper became inexpensive enough for everyone to use it, and origami then became a form of entertainment. Woodblock prints from this period show origami models, people folding paper, and origami shapes in kimono patterns.

In the 1890s, the Japanese government introduced a widespread system of preschool education, and origami was introduced as a tool for bringing minds and hands into coordination. It is still taught to young children today. Origami is now gaining respect as a valuable creative activity, receiving patronage from both Japanese industry and cultural institutions.

Origami and the Western world

The development of paper folding in the West can be traced back to a troupe of Japanese jugglers who visited Europe in the 1860s, soon after Japan's long period of isolation had ended with the Meiji restoration. The jugglers brought with them the method for folding the 'flapping bird'. Soon, directions for this and other folds were appearing in various European publications. Magicians including Harry Houdini and Robert Harbin were especially interested in paper folding, attesting to the link between origami and magic, which continues today.

Since the 1950s, interest in origami has proliferated in the United States and Great Britain as well as Japan, resulting in a variety of books and articles on the subject and in the founding of many origami societies worldwide (*see Useful Addresses, page 80*). Today, new and improved folding procedures have led to the creation of models that would have astounded the old origami masters. Where once it was considered almost impossible to fold a lifelike insect that gave the impression of a body, antennae and legs, anatomically correct ones are now considered commonplace. Happily, however, not all paper folders have reduced origami to achievements of technical skill. The artistry and purity of folding paper still flourishes.

Helpful Tips

Before you begin any of the projects in this book, read through the following tips designed to make origami easier.

- Before you start, make sure your paper is the correct shape.
- Do your folding on a smooth, flat surface such as a table or a book. Ensure that your folds are neat and accurate.
- Press your folds into place with your thumbnail.
- In the diagrams in this book, the shading represents the coloured side of the paper.
- Look at each diagram carefully, read the instructions, then look at the next diagram to see what shape should be created when you have completed the step you are working on.
- You will find it easiest to work your way through from the beginning of the book to the end, as some of the projects and procedures in later sections are based partially on previous ones. However, if you are an experienced paper folder and can follow origami instructions without too much help, feel free to select any design as a starting point.
- Most of the models can be folded from one square of paper, but a few require more. The instructions at the start of each project clearly state what you will need. If you are using your own paper rather than the paper supplied with this book, make sure it is cut absolutely square. There is nothing more frustrating than trying to fold a nearly square square!
- Above all, if a fold or whole model does not work out, don't give up hope. Go through the illustrations one by one, checking that you have read the instructions correctly. If you are still unable to complete the model, put it to one side and come back to it later with a fresh mind.

Symbols and the Basics of Folding

The symbols that form the basis of the instructions in this book are used internationally. They show the direction in which the paper should be folded. If you are new to origami, we suggest that you take a few squares of paper and study the following symbols and folding procedures before trying any of the origami projects. Look at the diagrams carefully to see which way the dashes, dots and arrows go over, through and under the paper, and fold your paper accordingly.

1 **Valley fold**

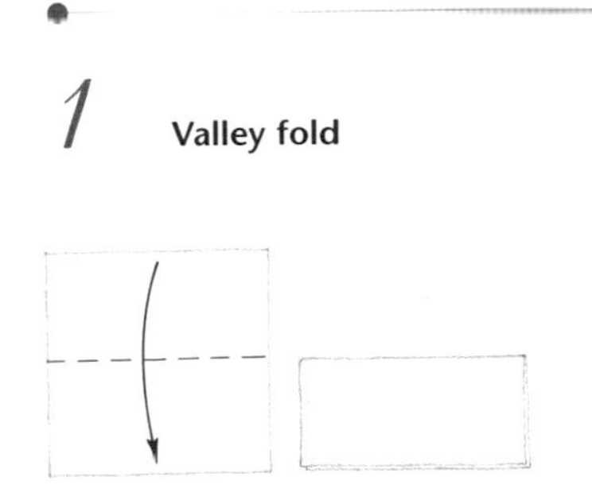

A valley fold (fold towards you or in front) is shown by a line of dashes and a solid arrow showing the direction in which the paper has to be folded.

2 **Mountain fold**

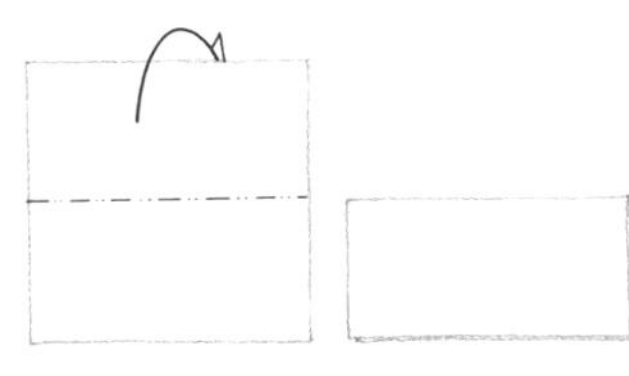

A mountain fold (fold away from you or behind) is shown by a line of dots and dashes and a hollow-headed arrow. As in the valley fold, the arrow shows the direction in which the paper has to be folded.

3 **Fold and unfold**

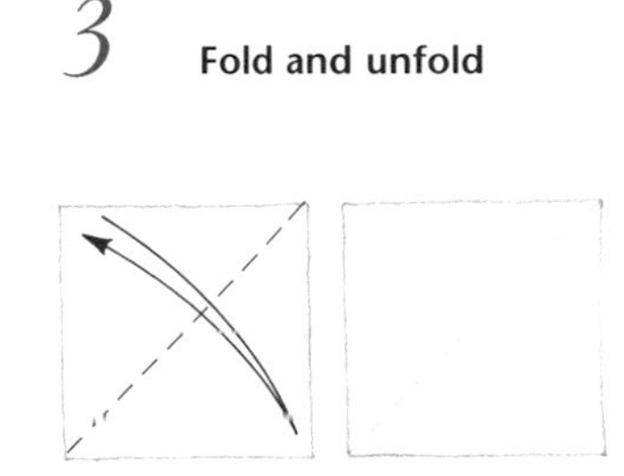

An arrow that comes back on itself means fold, press flat and unfold the paper back to its previous position.

4 Step fold

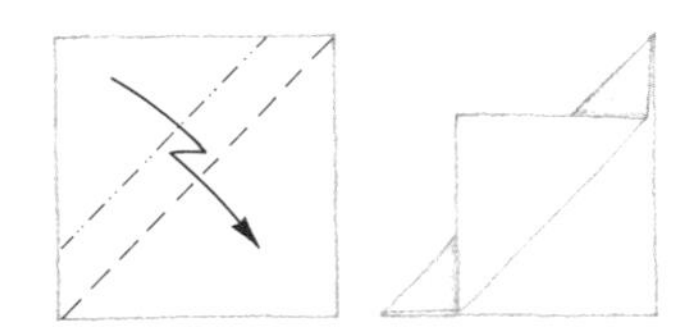

A zigzagged arrow drawn on top of the diagram means fold the paper in the direction shown by the arrow. A step fold is made by pleating the paper in a valley and mountain fold.

5 Fold over and over

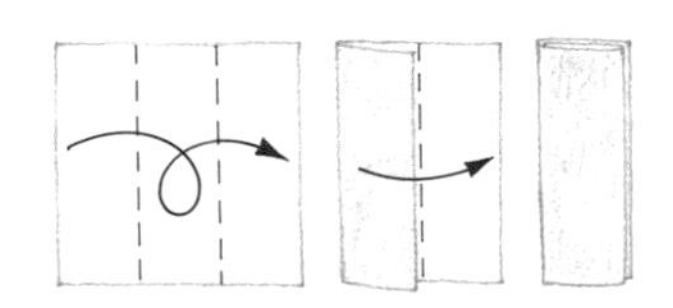

A looped arrow drawn on top of a diagram means keep folding the paper over in the direction shown by the arrow. Each fold-line represents one fold-over move.

6 Outside reverse fold

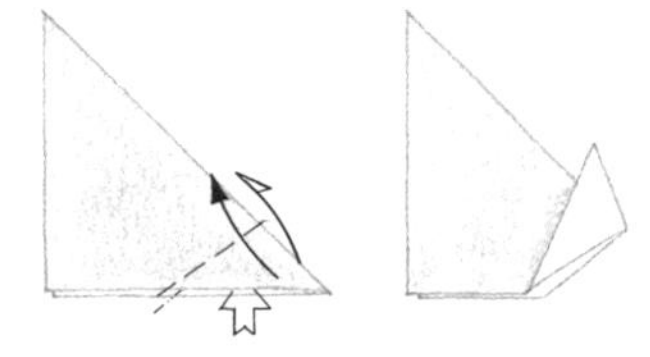

Solid and hollow-headed arrows, and valley and mountain fold-lines instruct you to separate the layers of paper, taking one to the front and one to the back.

10 Turn around

Two circling arrows means turn the paper (or model) around into the position shown.

11 Cut

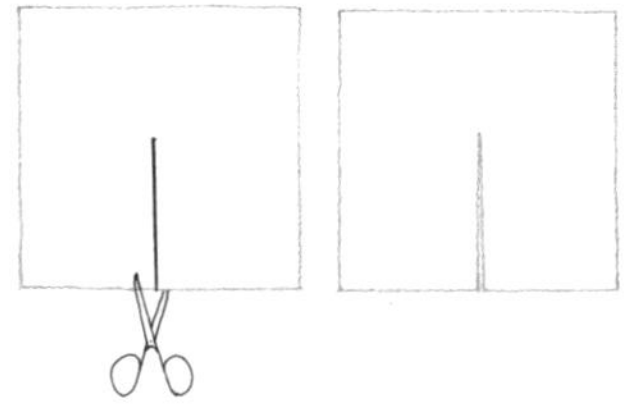

A pair of scissors and a solid line means cut the paper. The solid line shows the position of the cut.

12 Insert

An arrow with the tail broken near the head means insert the point into the pocket as shown.

7 Inside reverse fold

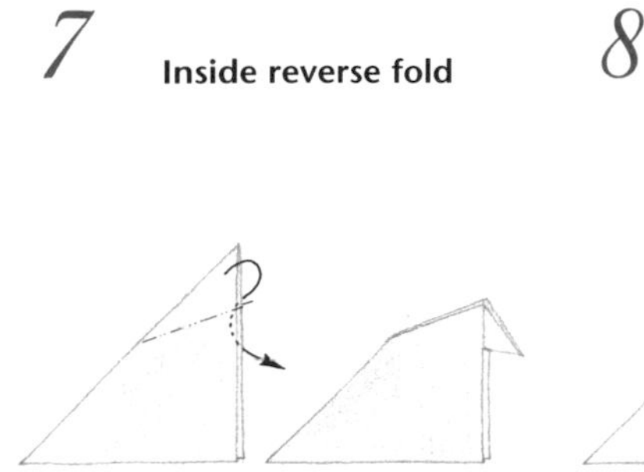

A wavy arrow with a broken tail and a mountain fold-line means pull the point inside the model, in the direction indicated by the wavy arrow.

8 Open and squash

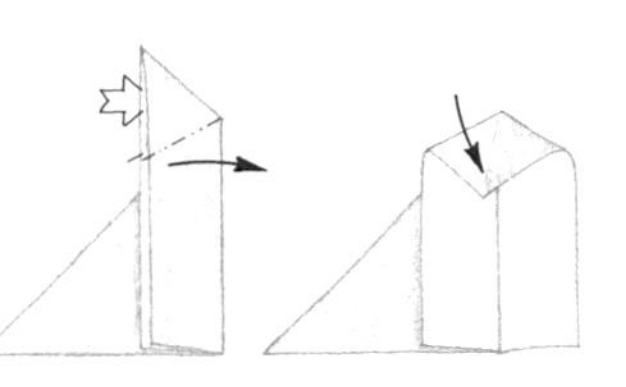

A hollow arrow with a short, indented tail instructs you to open out the layers of paper and squash them down neatly into the position shown in the following diagram.

9 Turn over

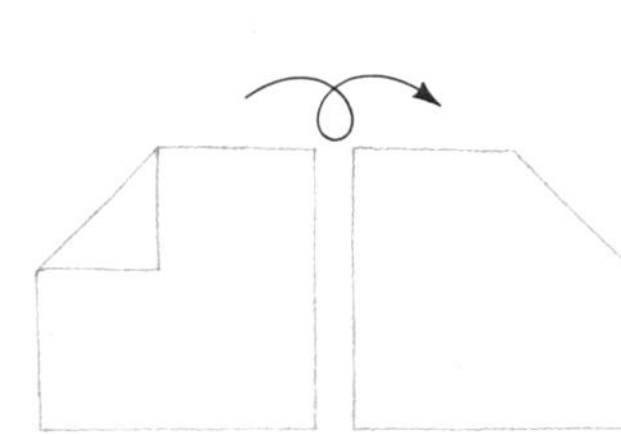

A looped arrow means turn the paper (or model) over in the direction shown.

13 Blow

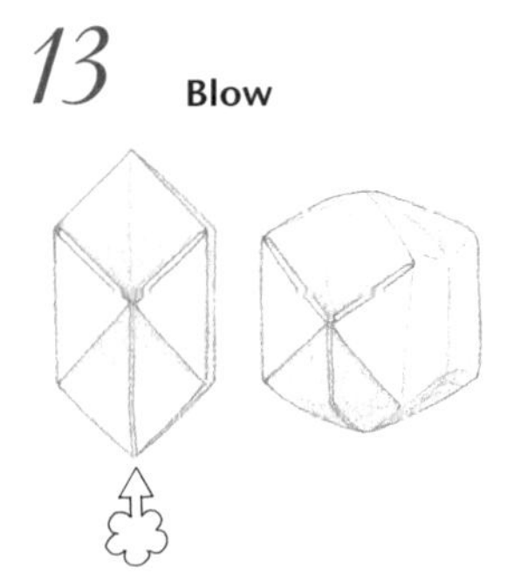

A hollow arrow with a cloud-like tail instructs you to blow where the arrow indicates. This symbol is used when a particular fold has to be inflated …

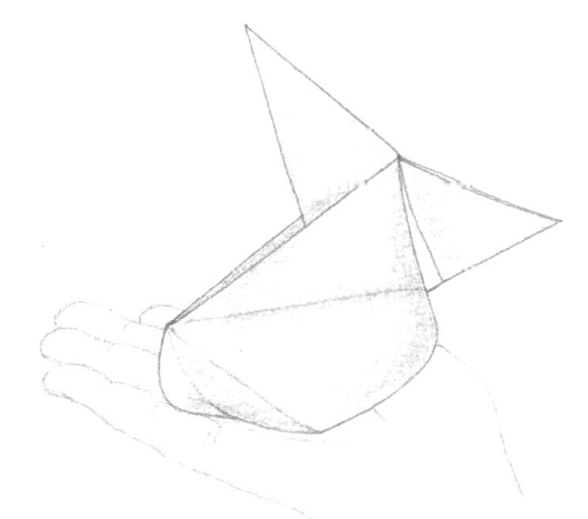

... for example the goldfish

Goldfish

Making Your Goldfish

This captivating origami model is thought to have originated in China. Use a square piece of paper, white side up.

1

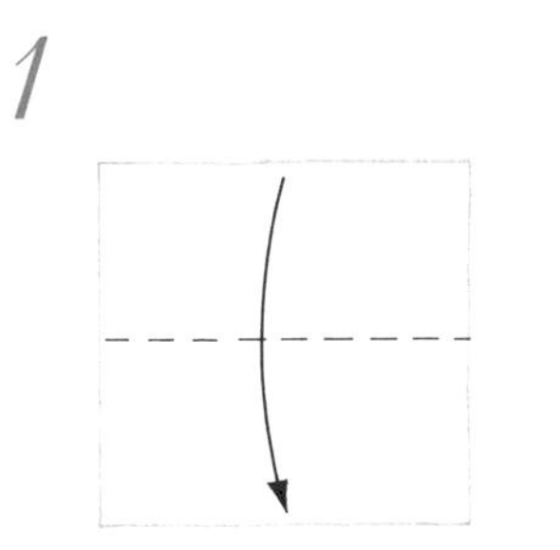

Valley fold the square in half from top to bottom.

2

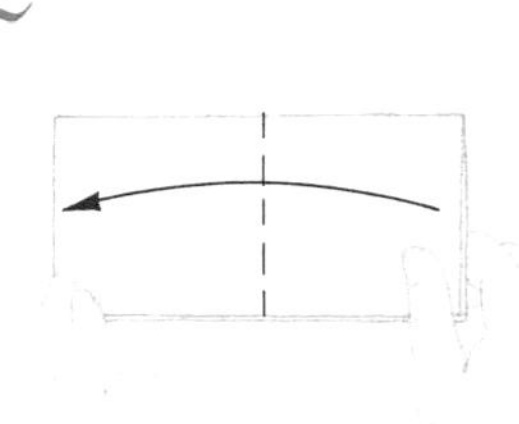

Valley fold the paper in half from right to left.

3

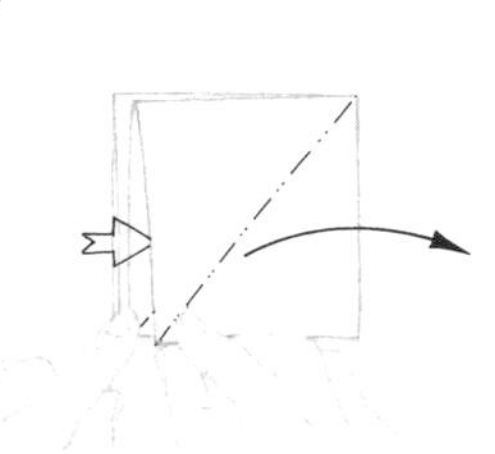

Lift the top half up, open out the paper and ...

4

... squash it down neatly ...

5

... into a triangle.

6

Turn the paper over. Repeat steps 2 to 5, to make a waterbomb base.

7

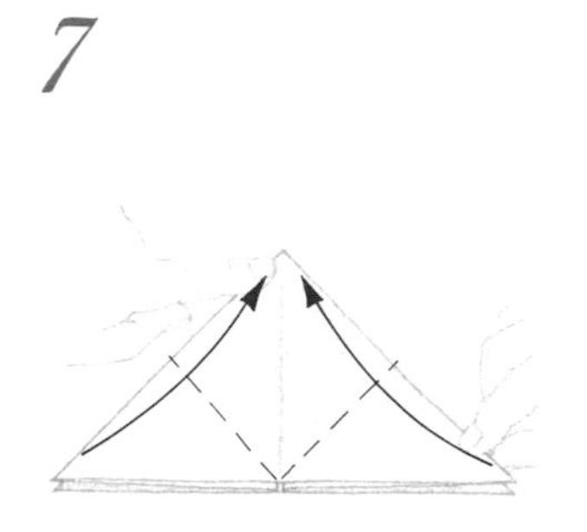

Take the top layer and valley fold the bottom points up to meet the top point.

8

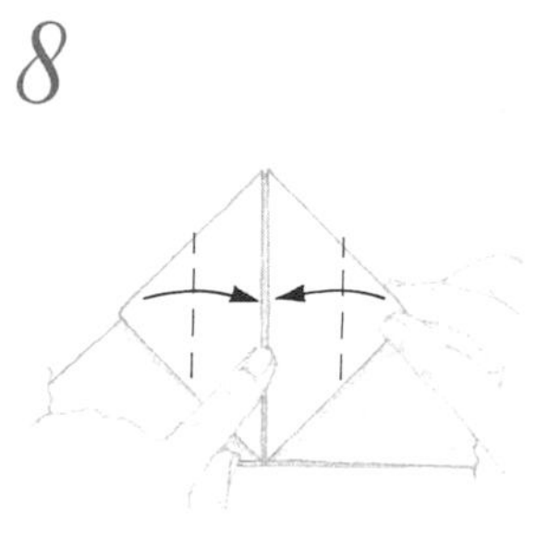

Valley fold the side points in to the middle.

9

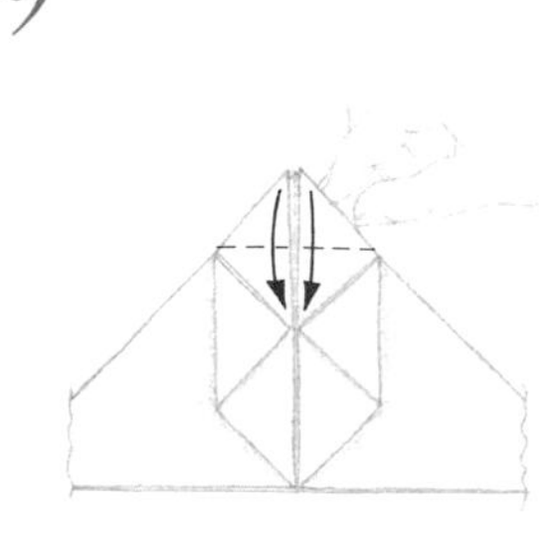

Valley fold the top points in to the middle, to make two triangular flaps at the top.

13

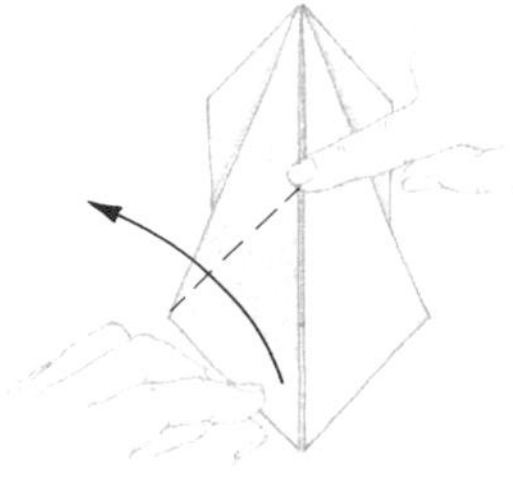

Valley fold the bottom left-hand fin over and outward into the position shown in step 14.

14

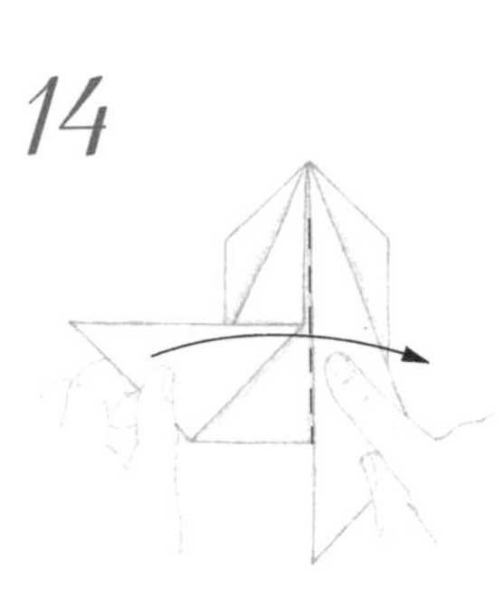

Valley fold the left-hand fin over to the right, as though turning the page of a book.

15

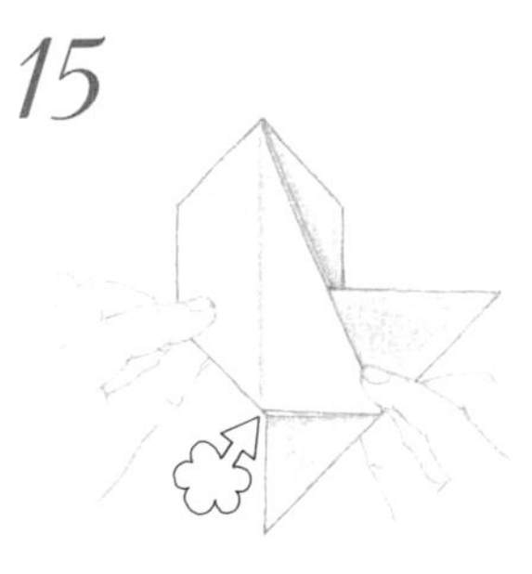

Hold the paper between fingers and thumbs with the small hole that is located at the base of the fins facing you. Place your lips right up to the paper and blow gently into the hole, which ...

10

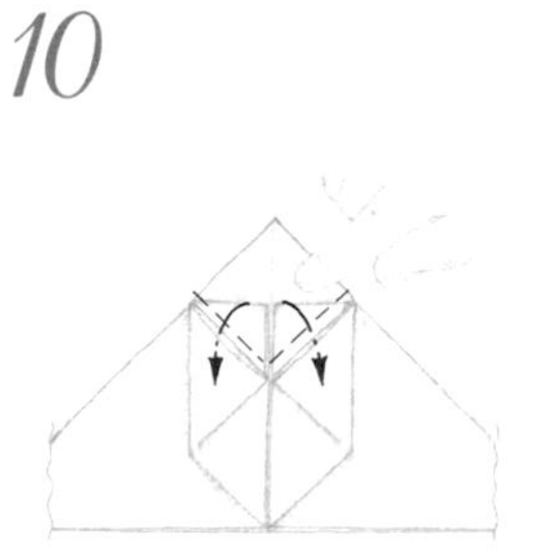

Tuck these flaps into the adjacent pockets with a valley fold.

11

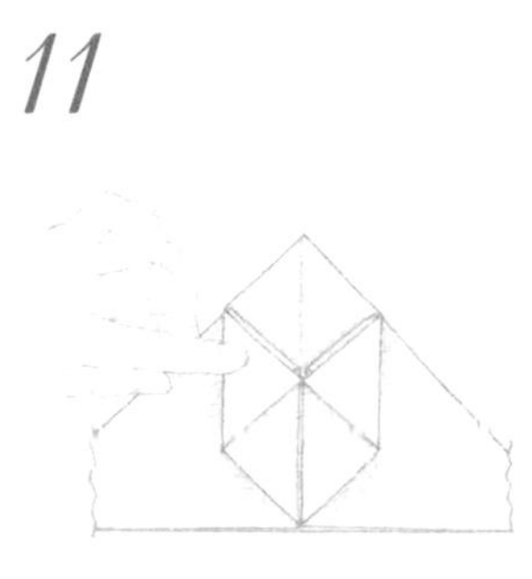

Your model should now look like this.

12

Turn the paper over. From the top point, valley fold the sloping edges in to meet the middle fold-line, making the tail fins.

16

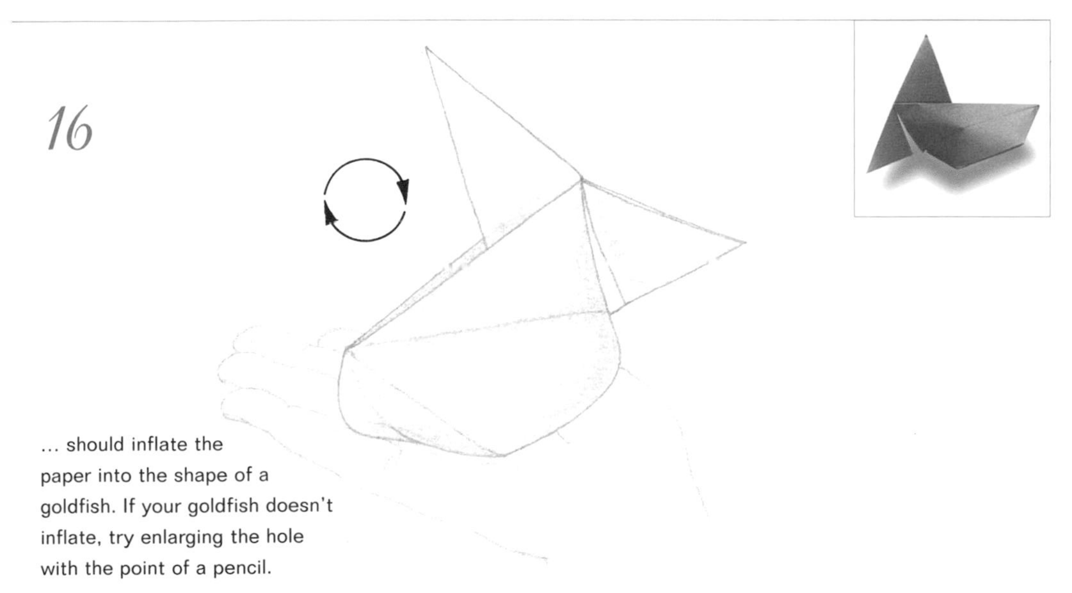

... should inflate the paper into the shape of a goldfish. If your goldfish doesn't inflate, try enlarging the hole with the point of a pencil.

Mandarin Duck

Making Your Mandarin Duck

The following model should help you to understand inside and outside reverse folds. Use a square piece of paper, coloured side up.

1

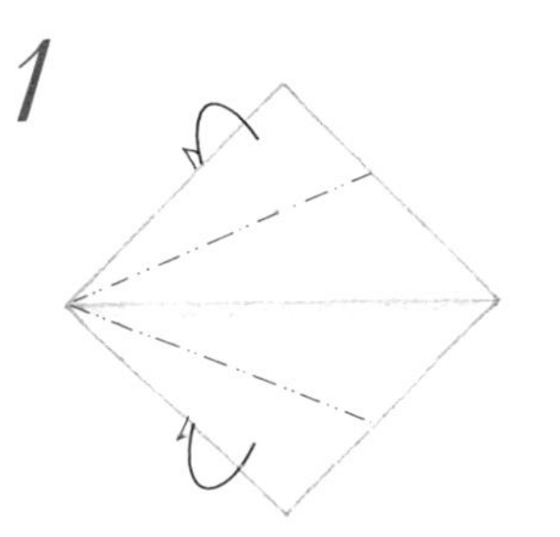

Crease the middle fold-line as shown. From the left-hand point, mountain fold the sloping edges behind to meet the middle fold-line, making a kite base.

2

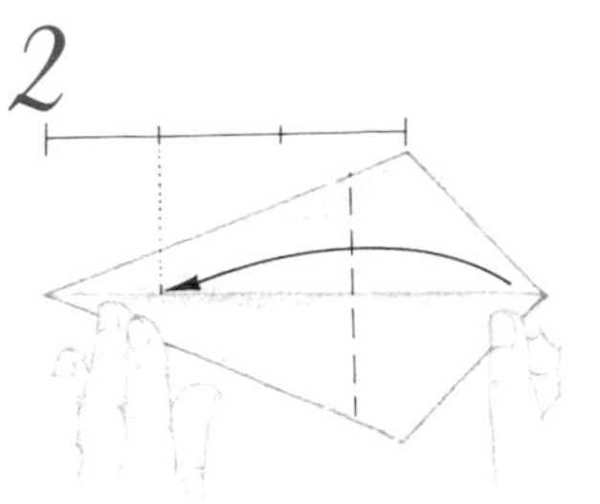

Valley fold the right-hand point over to the left as far as shown.

3

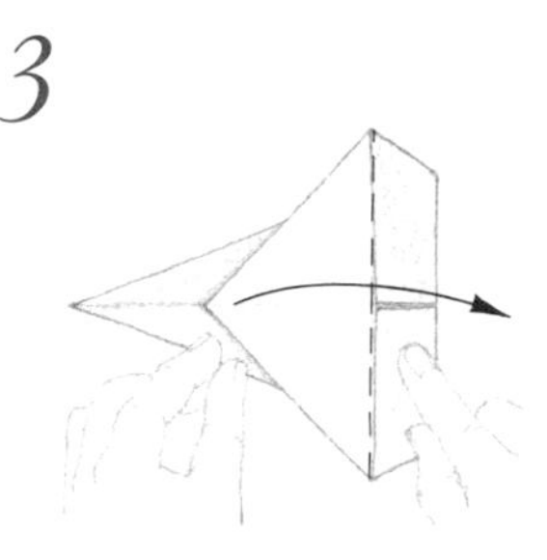

Valley fold the point back out to the right.

4

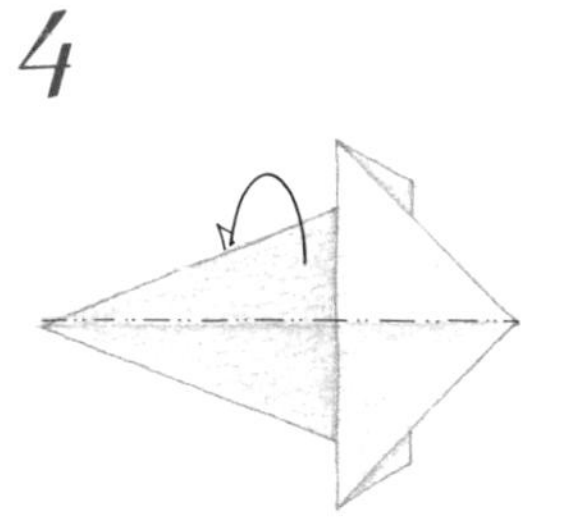

Mountain fold the paper in half from top to bottom.

5

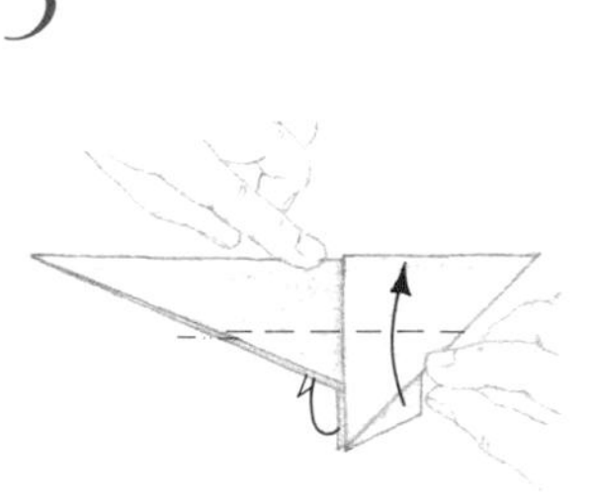

Valley fold the bottom point up, to make a wing. Repeat behind.

6

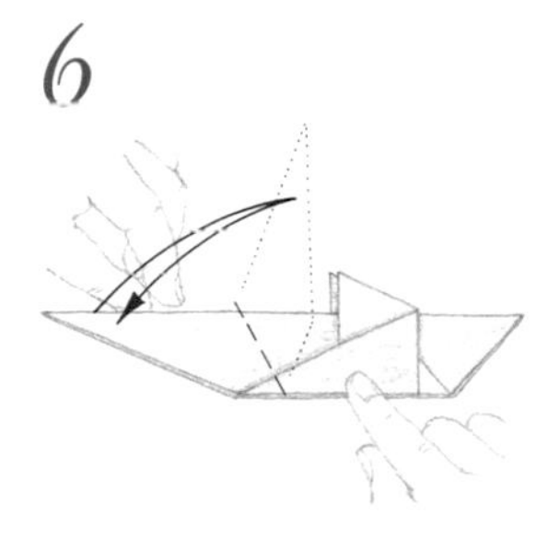

Fold and unfold the left-hand point into the position shown by the dotted lines.

7

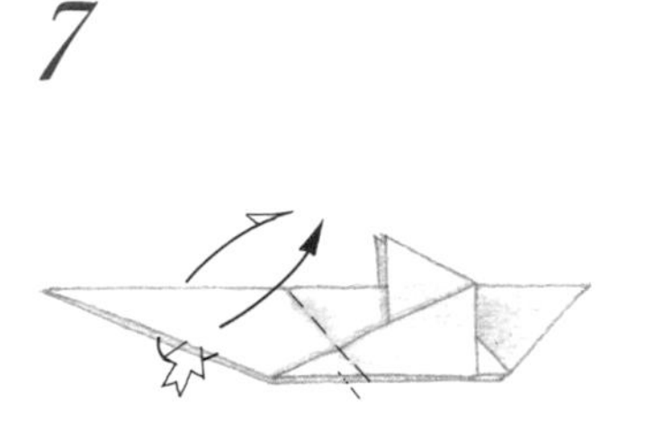

Outside reverse fold the left-hand point along the fold-lines made in step 6.

8

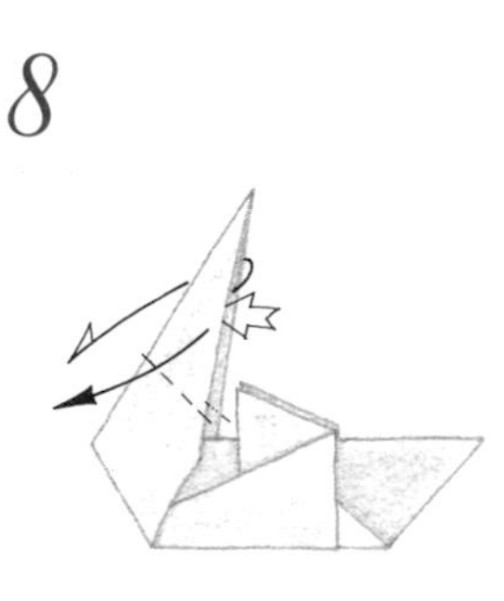

Again, outside reverse fold the point, so it points to the left, making the duck's head and beak.

9

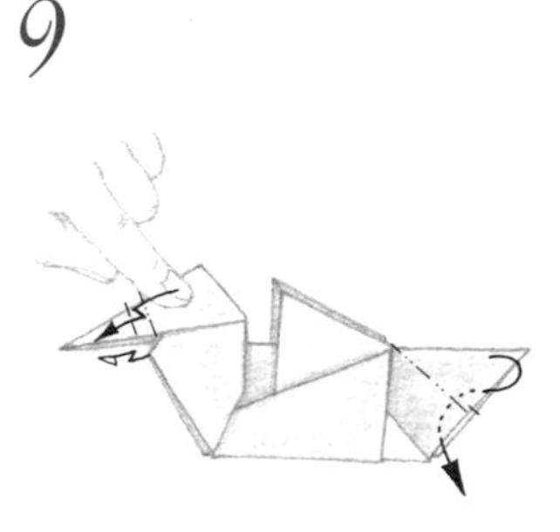

Step fold the beak on either side as shown. Inside reverse fold the right-hand point down.

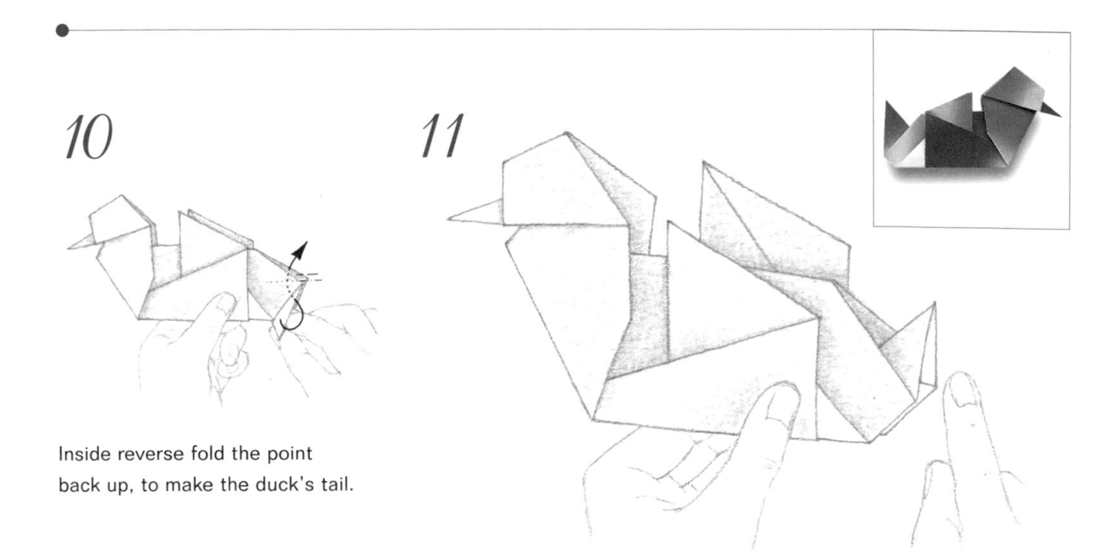

10

Inside reverse fold the point back up, to make the duck's tail.

11

Your mandarin duck is complete.

Lily Pad and Frog

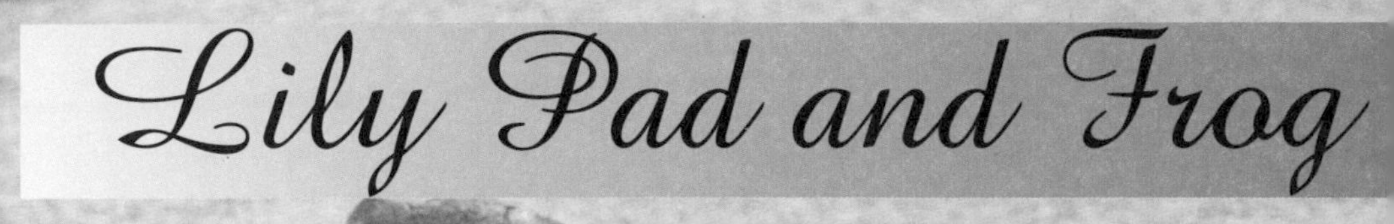

Making Your Lily Pad and Frog

The lily pad is a very simple model, based upon a Japanese paper-cutting technique called *kirigami*. The leaf looks perfect when it is displayed alongside the frog and lotus flower. Use two squares of paper, equal in size. You will also need a pair of scissors.

1

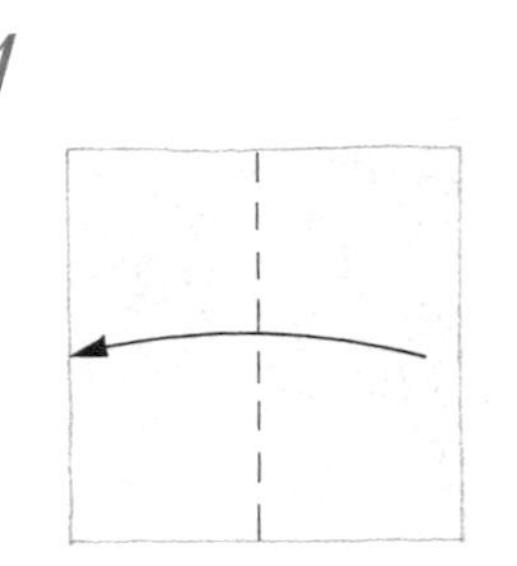

To make the lily pad:
Valley fold one square in half from right to left, with the coloured side on top.

2

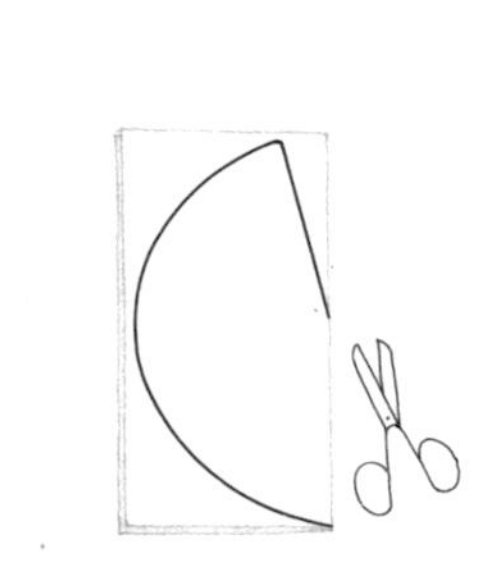

From the folded edge, cut out the lily pad shape as shown.

3

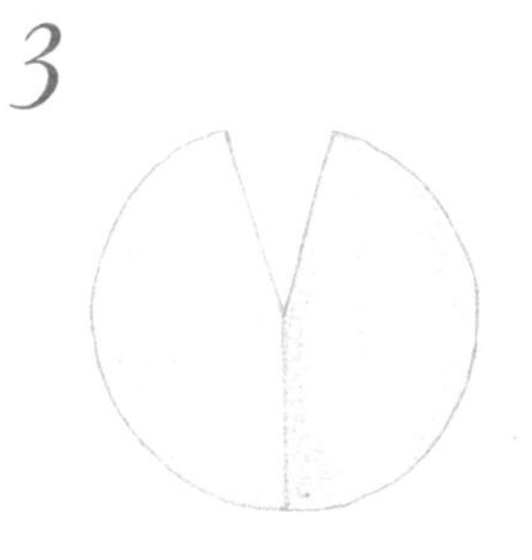

To complete the lily pad, unfold the paper.

7

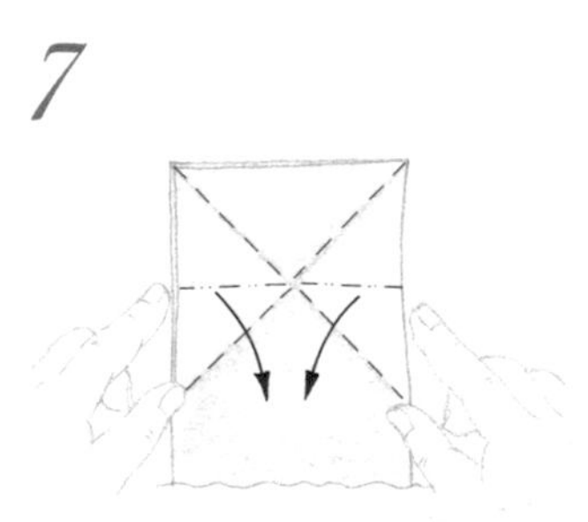

Bring the sides together and down towards you along the fold-lines made in steps 5 and 6.

8

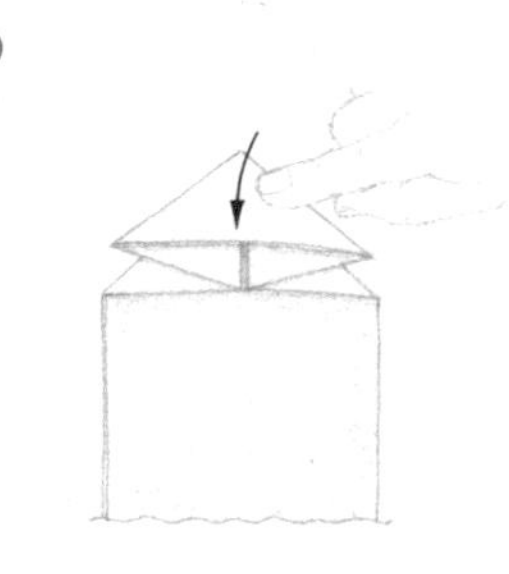

Press the top down neatly into a triangle.

9

Valley fold the bottom edge up to meet the triangle's base.

4

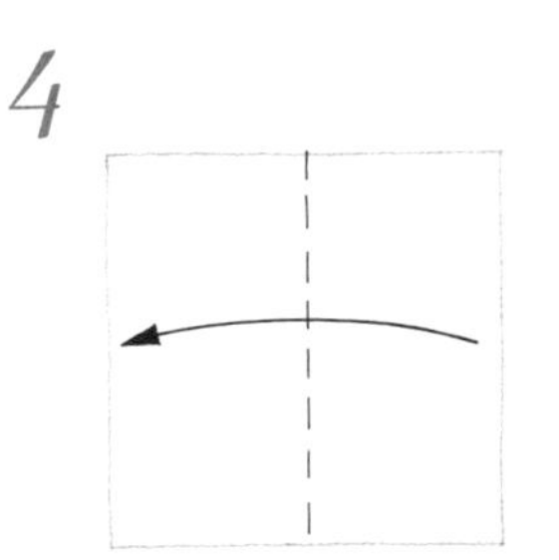

To make the frog:
Valley fold the remaining square in half from right to left, with the white side on top.

5

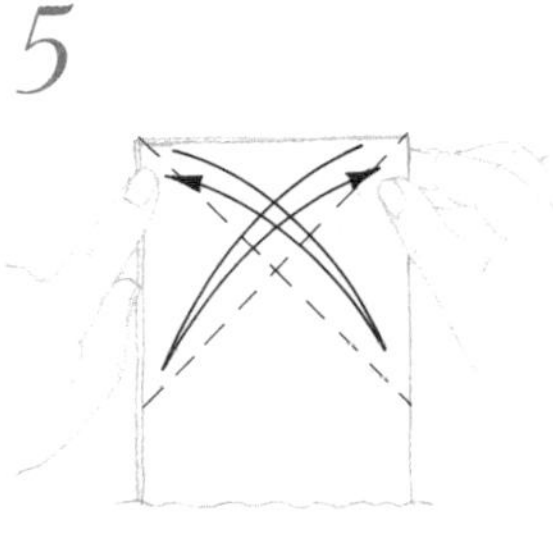

Fold and unfold the top part of the paper as shown.

6

Fold and unfold the top edge behind as shown.

10

Valley fold the sides in to meet the middle, leaving behind the top layers of the triangle.

11

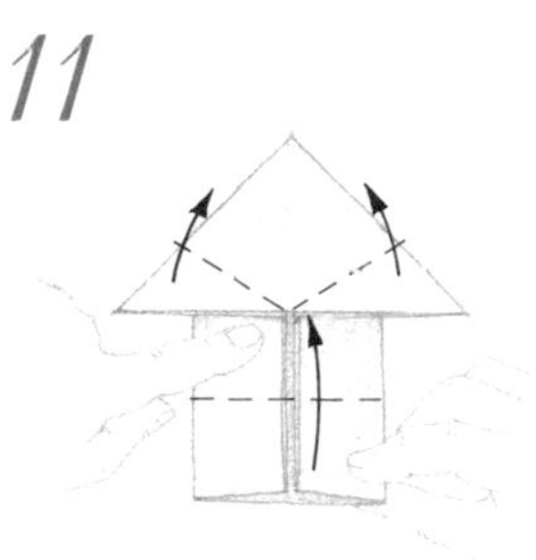

Valley fold the bottom edge as shown. Valley fold the triangle's bottom points out from the middle, to make the front legs.

12

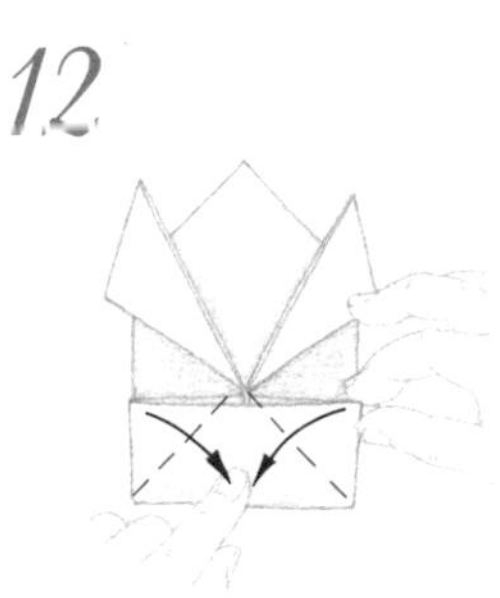

Valley fold the bottom flap's top corners down to meet the bottom edge.

13

Pinch both sides of the point and pull the outer layers apart, into the position shown in step 14. Press the paper flat.

14

Valley fold the two triangular flaps down.

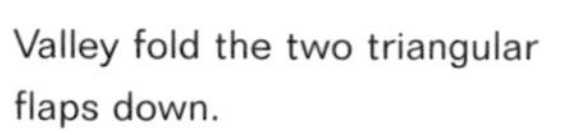

15

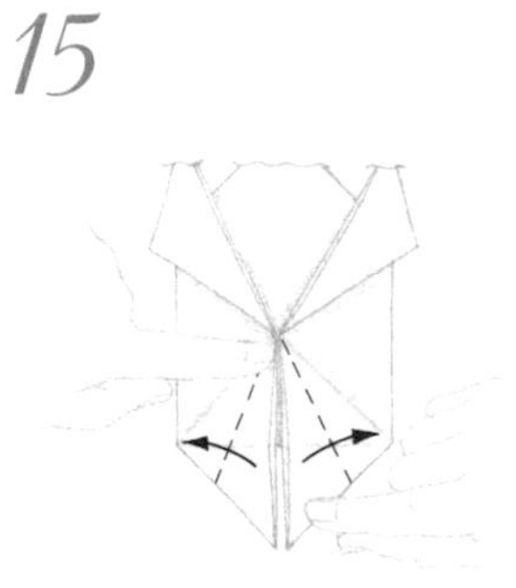

Valley fold the flaps out from the middle, to make the frog's back legs.

16

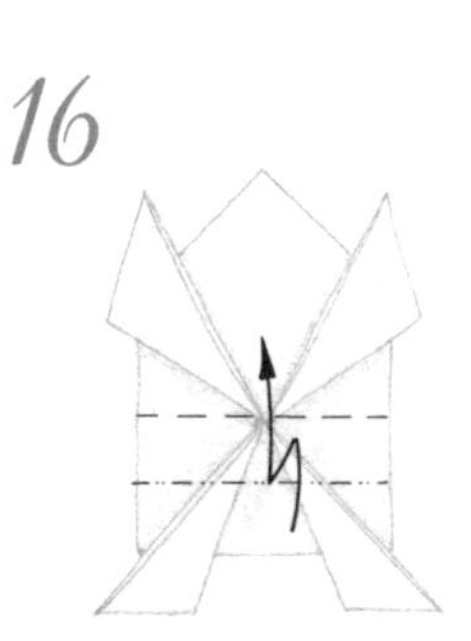

Step fold the bottom section of paper as shown.

17

The frog is finished. If you place him on a flat surface and press firmly on the base of his back, he will jump up into the air and may even turn a complete somersault.

Lotus Flower

Making Your Lotus Flower

Be very careful not to tear the paper when folding this pretty flower. If you make your lotus flower out of a starched cloth napkin, it will make a perfect table decoration. To begin with, practise with a white square of paper.

1

Crease the middle fold-lines as shown.

2

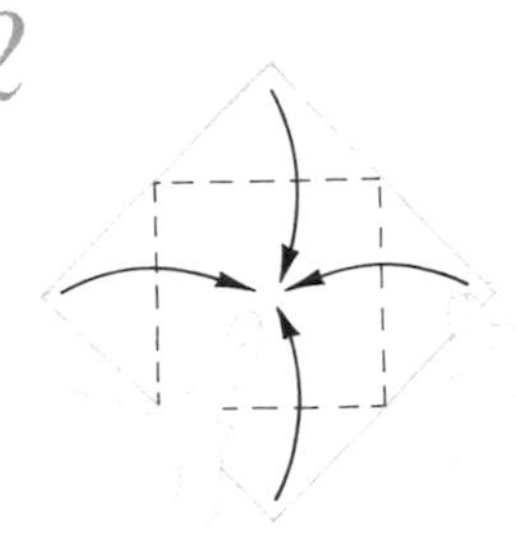

Valley fold the corners in to meet the middle, making a blintz base.

3

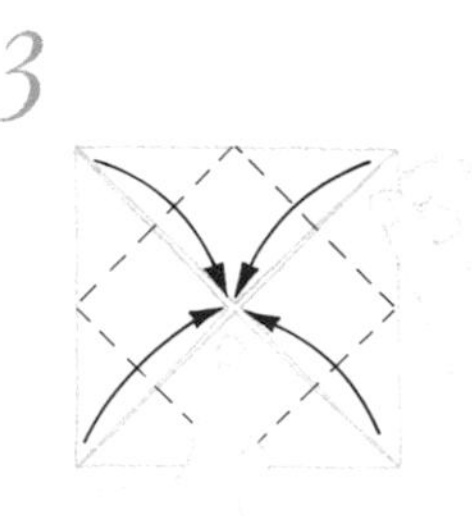

Again, valley fold the corners in to meet the middle.

7

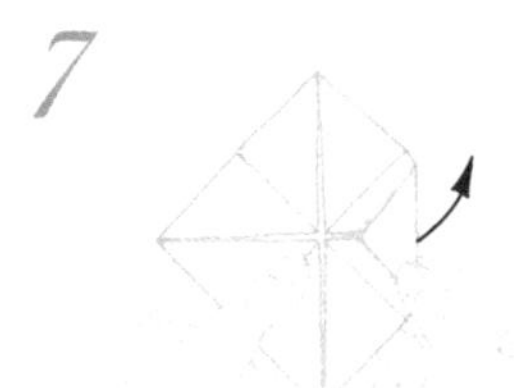

From the top layer of paper, pull over a corner from behind. Stand the corner upright and shape it to look like a petal.

8

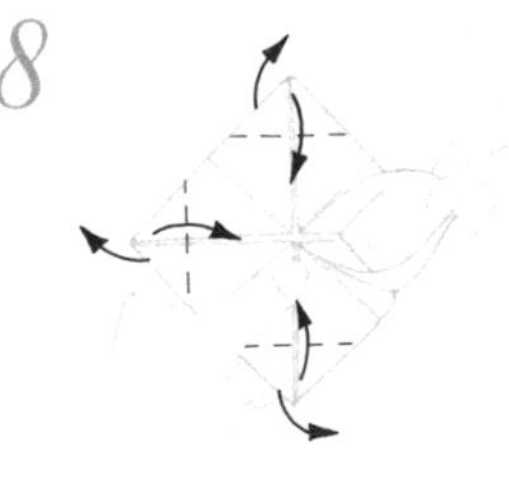

Repeat steps 6 and 7 with the remaining three corners, to make the first layer of petals.

9

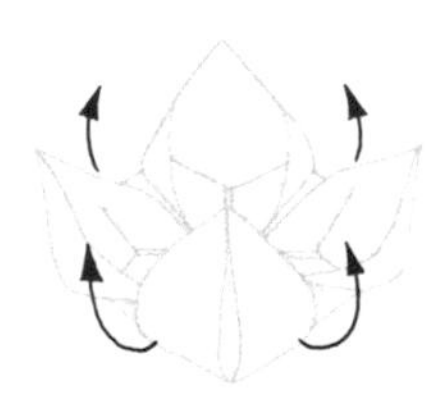

Pull over from behind the four corners from the next layer of paper, to make the second layer of petals.

4

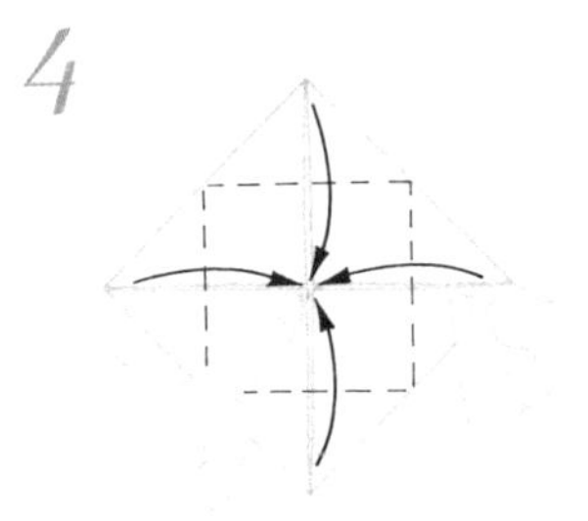

And again, valley fold the corners in to the middle. The result is three layers each comprising four corners.

5

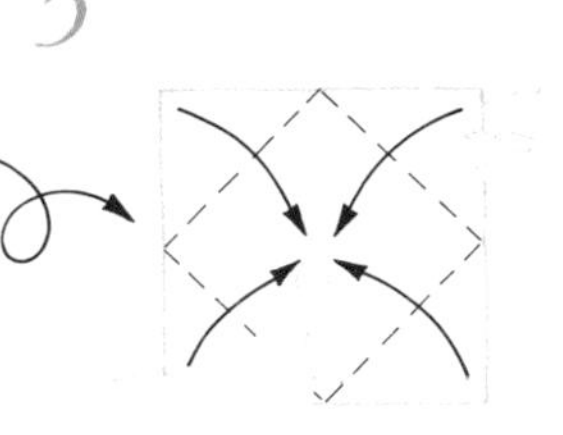

Turn the paper over. For the last time, valley fold the corners in to meet the middle.

6

Valley fold over a little of one corner.

10

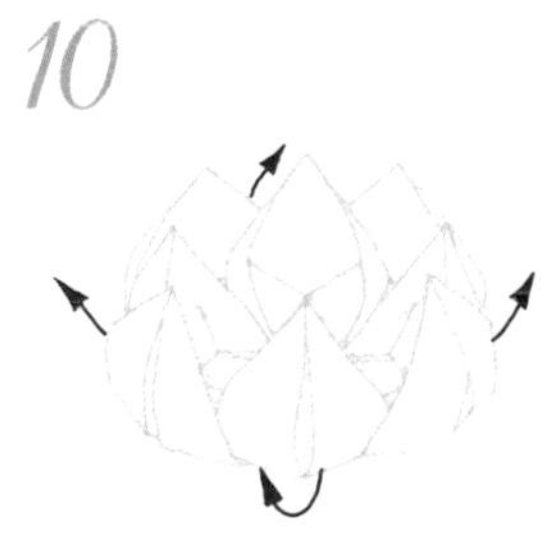

Pull over from behind the four corners from the final layer of paper, to make the third layer of petals.

11

The lotus flower is especially effective when combined with the lily pad and frog.

Crane

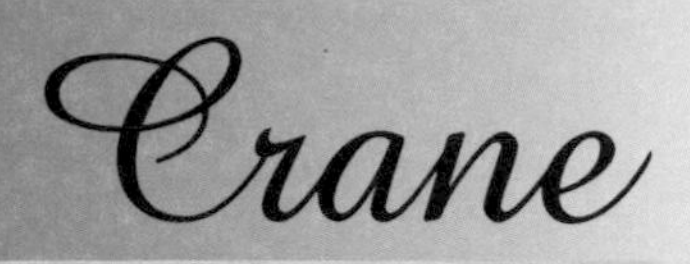

Making Your Crane

If you fold a thousand cranes within one year of your life and string them together, it is believed to confer longevity on you the creator, and to wish the recipient a long life and sustained good health. Use a square piece of paper, white side up.

1

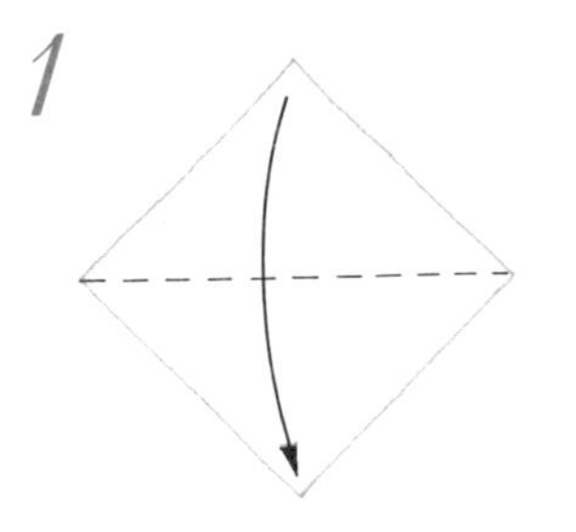

Turn the square around to look like a diamond. Valley fold it in half from top to bottom, to make a diaper fold.

2

Valley fold the paper in half from right to left.

3

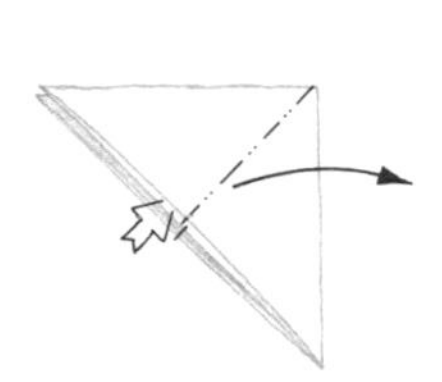

Lift the top layer up. Open out the paper and ...

4

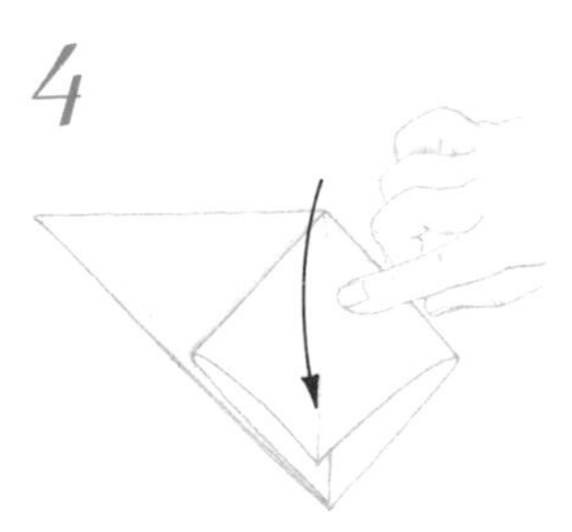

... squash it down neatly into a diamond.

5

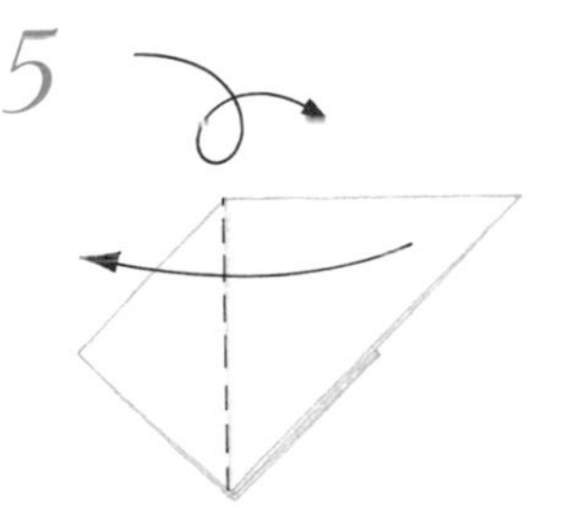

Turn the paper over. Repeat steps 2 to 4, to make a preliminary fold.

6

Fold and unfold the lower sloping edges (top half only) as shown.

7

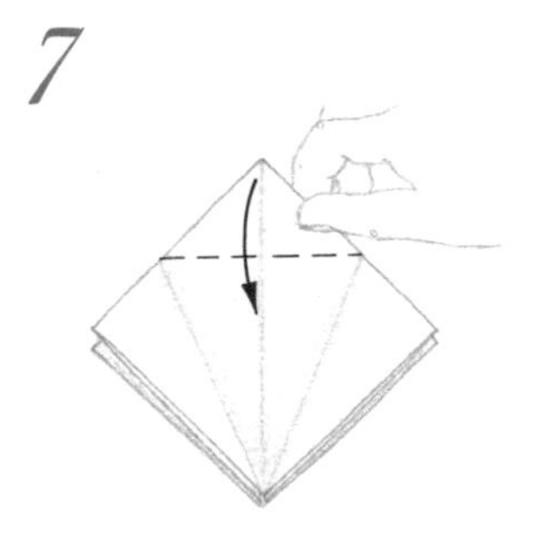

Valley fold the top point down as shown.

8

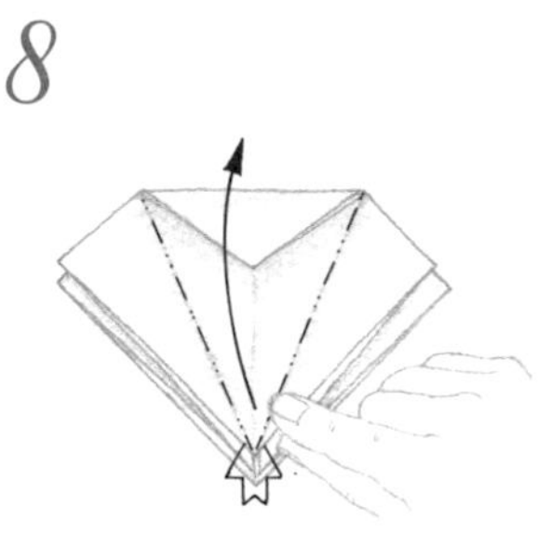

Now, to make a petal fold, pinch and lift up the front flap of paper.

9

Continue to lift the flap up until its edges meet along the middle line.

13

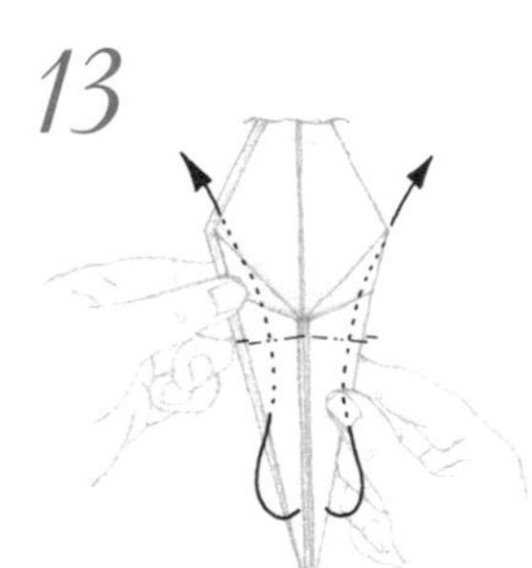

Inside reverse fold the bottom points.

14

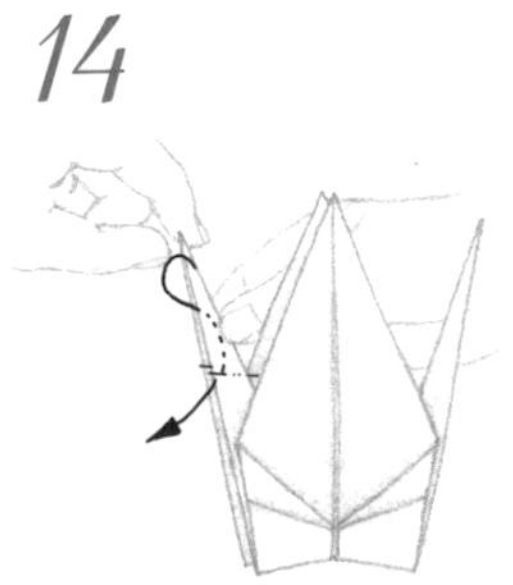

Inside reverse fold the tip of one of the points, to make the crane's head and beak.

15

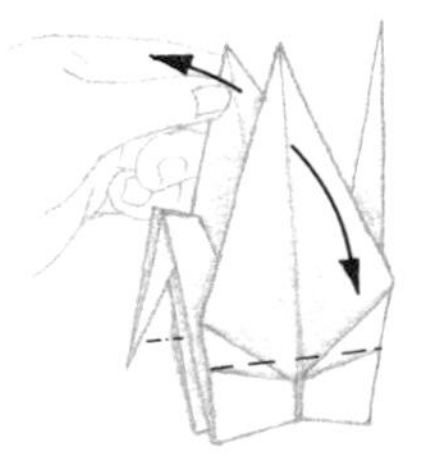

Fold the wings down slightly.

10

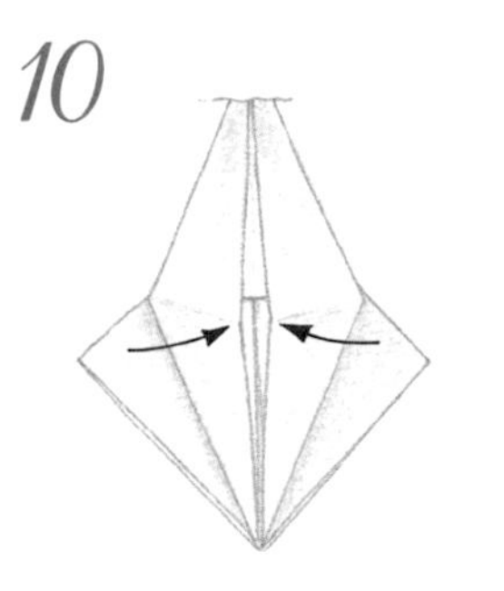

Press the paper flat to form a diamond shape. This completes the petal fold.

11

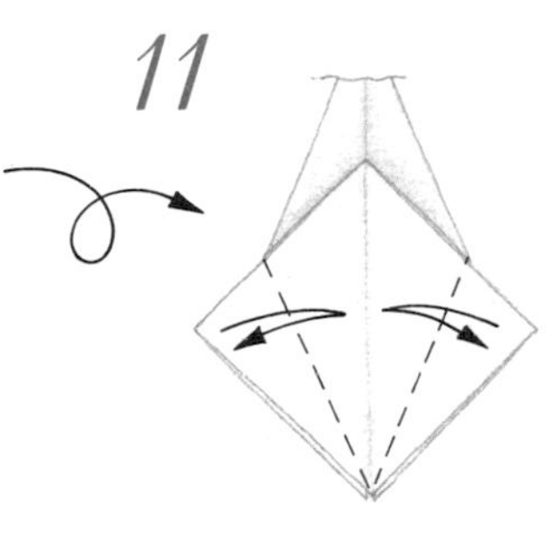

Turn the paper over. Repeat steps 6 to 10, to make a bird base.

12

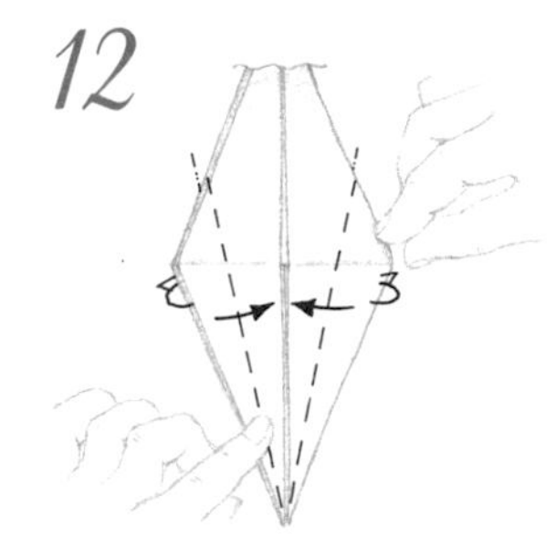

Valley fold the lower sloping edges (top layer only), so they lie along the middle line. Turn the paper over and repeat.

16

17

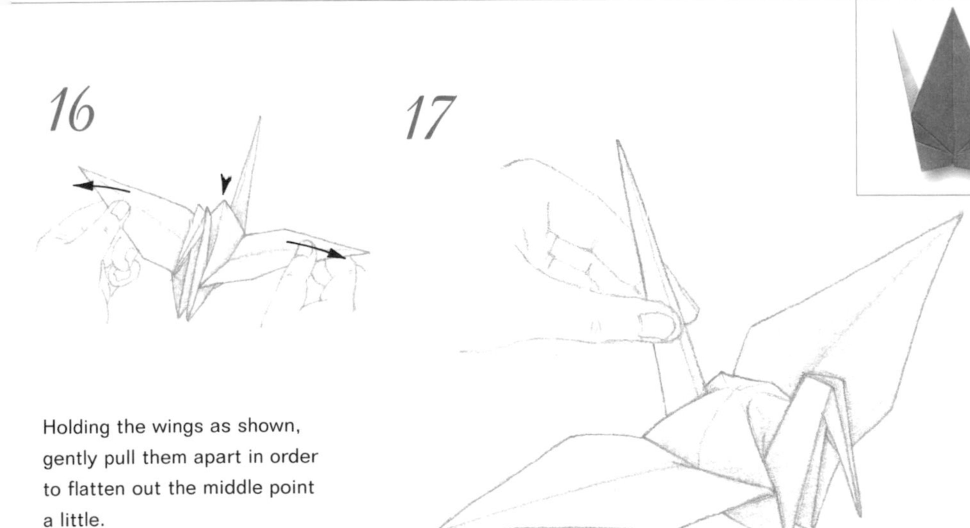

Holding the wings as shown, gently pull them apart in order to flatten out the middle point a little.

The completed crane.

Monkey

Making Your Monkey

Try changing the angle of the folds in step 7 each time you make this model, to see how many different expressions you can give your monkeys. Use a square piece of paper, white side up.

1

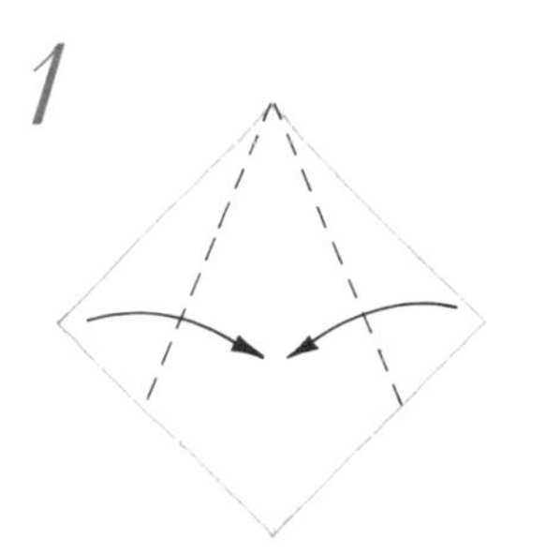

Crease the middle fold-line as shown. From the top point, valley fold the edges in to the middle fold-line, to make a kite base.

2

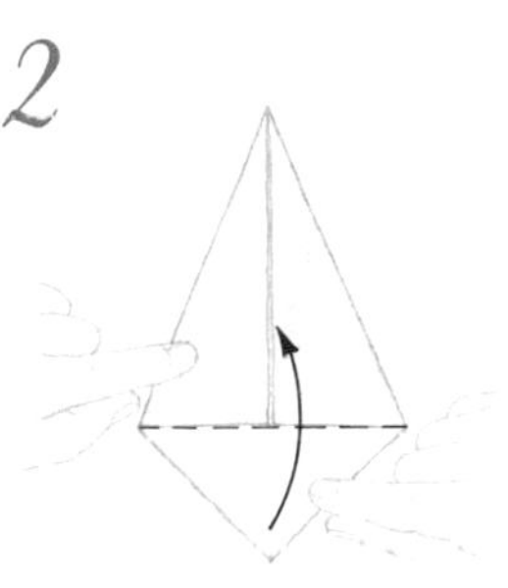

Valley fold the bottom point up on a line between the two side points.

3

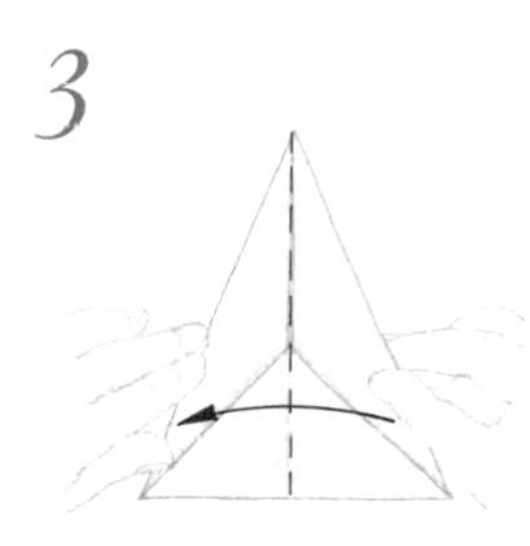

Valley fold the paper in half from right to left.

4

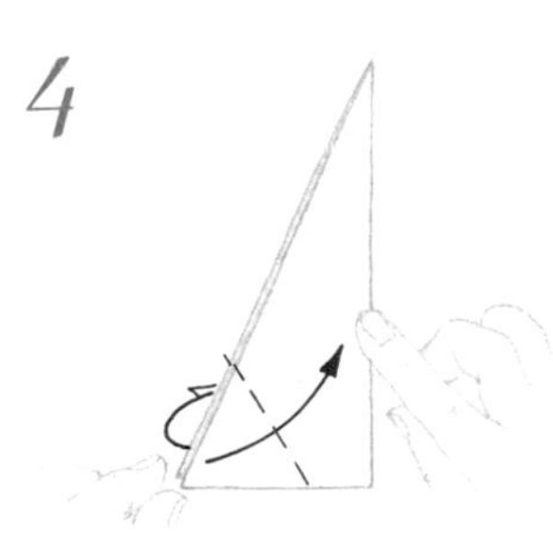

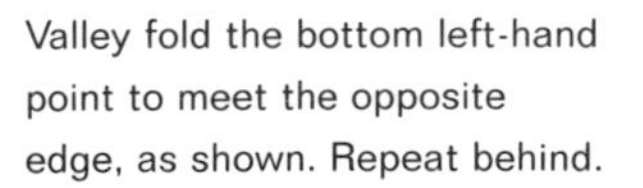

Valley fold the bottom left-hand point to meet the opposite edge, as shown. Repeat behind.

5

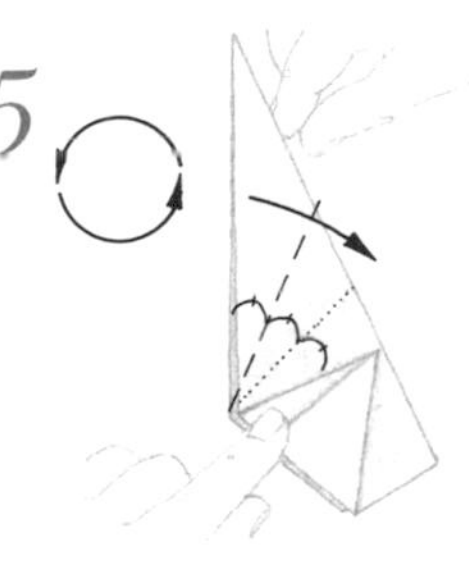

Turn the paper around a little. Valley fold the left-hand edges over as far as shown.

6

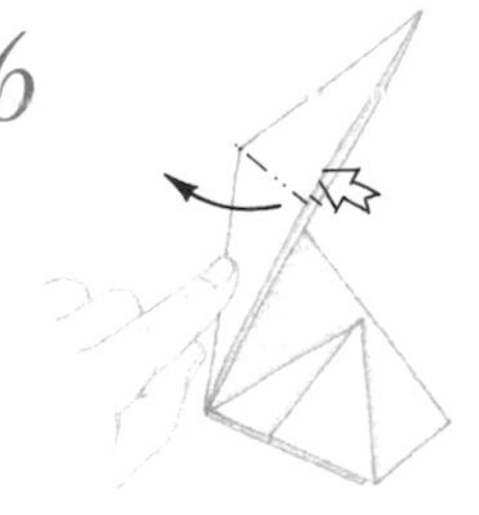

Open out the point and squash it down neatly into the position shown in step 7, to make the monkey's face.

7

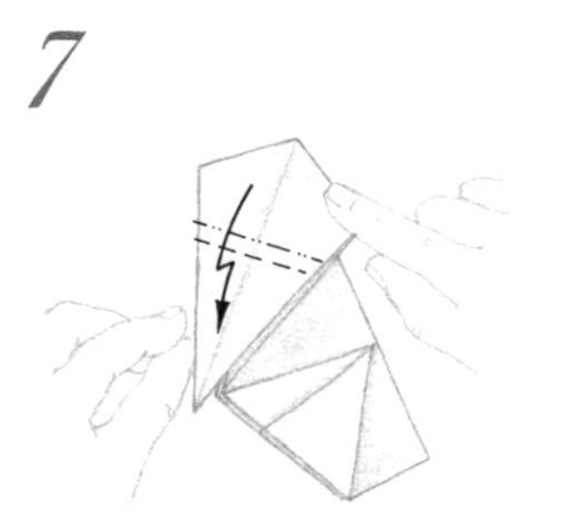

Shape the face with a step fold as shown.

8

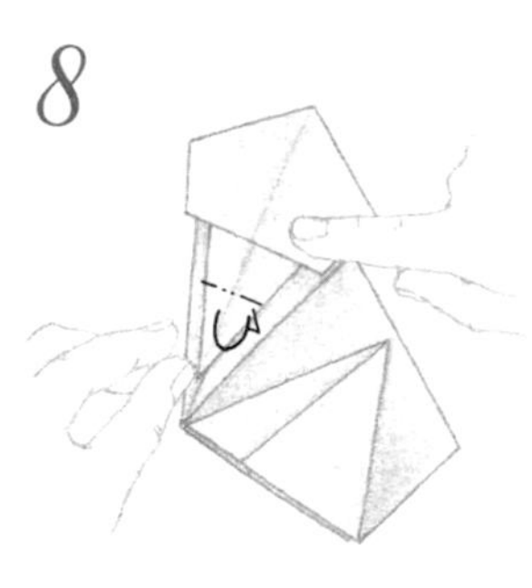

Mountain fold the tip of the face, up inside the model.

9

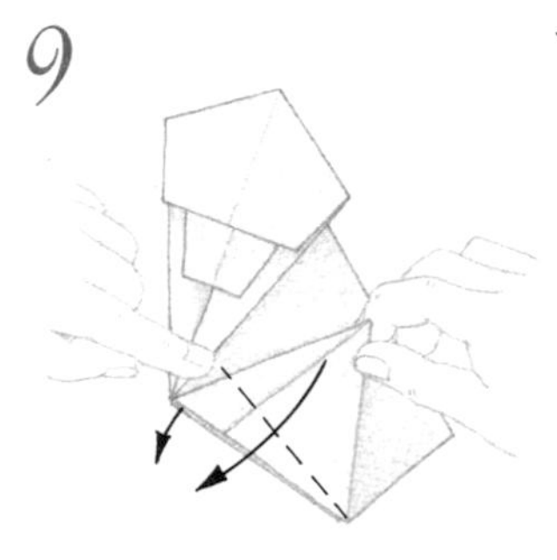

Valley fold the front point down, to make a leg. Repeat behind.

10

11

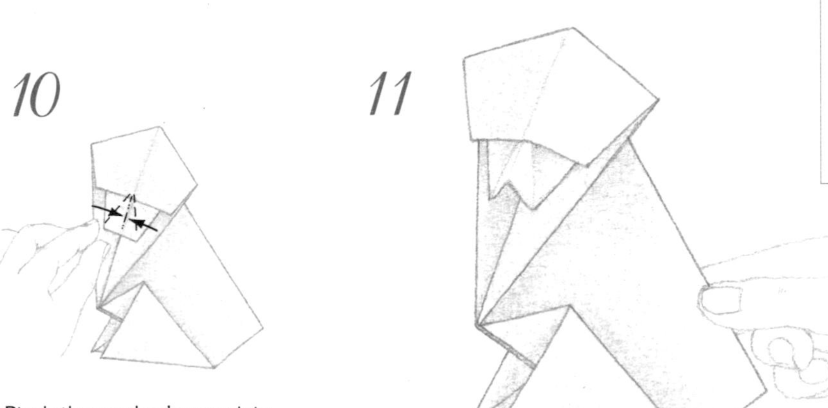

Pinch the monkey's nose into shape.

Your monkey is complete.

Rooster

Making Your Rooster

Steps 8, 13 and 14 of this model are a bit tricky, so do take your time folding them. Use a square piece of paper, coloured side up

1

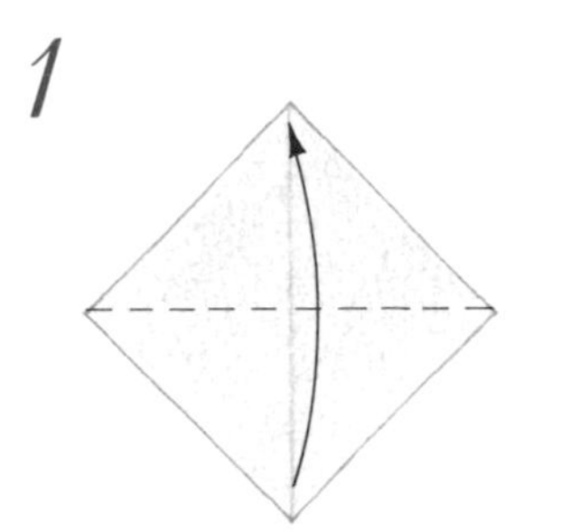

Crease the middle fold-line as shown. Valley fold the paper in half from bottom to top.

2

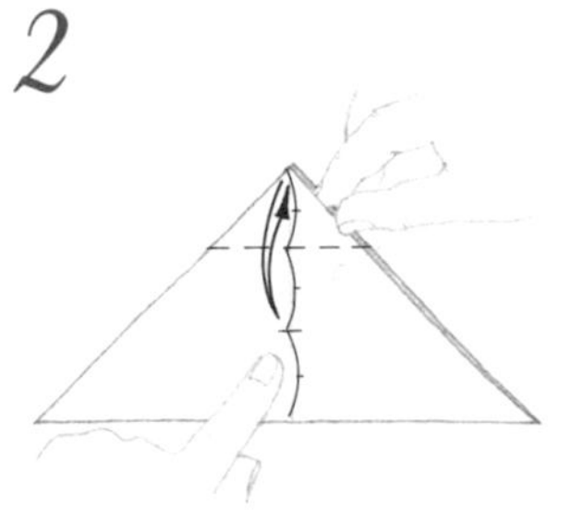

Fold and unfold the top point (upper layer only) as shown.

3

Fold and unfold the top point's sloping edges (upper layer only) to meet the fold-line made in step 2.

7

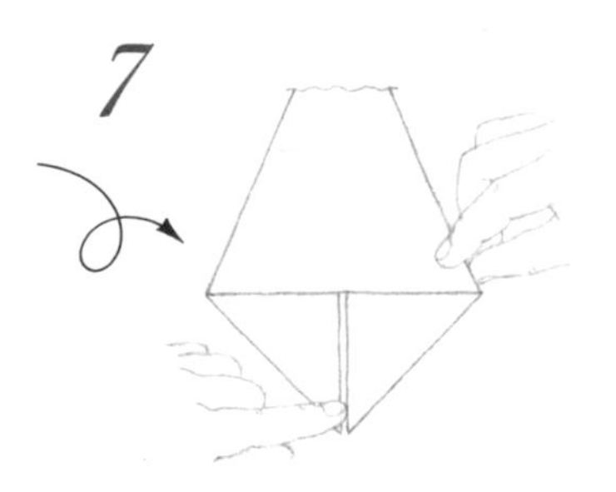

Turn the paper over. From the bottom point, fold and unfold the sloping edges in to meet the middle line.

8

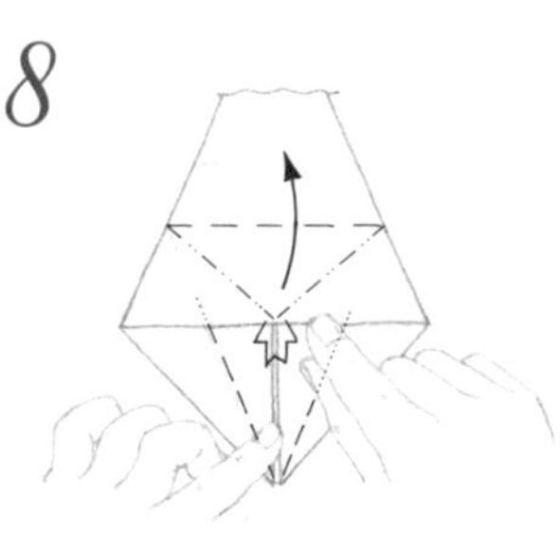

Pinch and lift the horizontal edge, so that the sloping edges fold in along the fold-lines made in step 7, and meet the middle line.

9

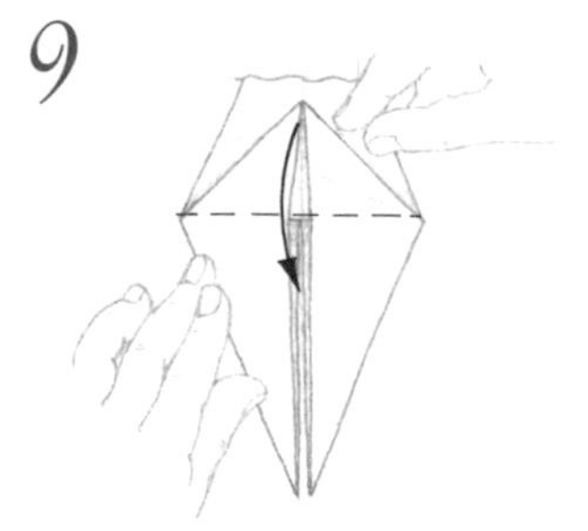

Press the paper down neatly to make a triangular flap. Valley fold the flap down as far as it will go.

4

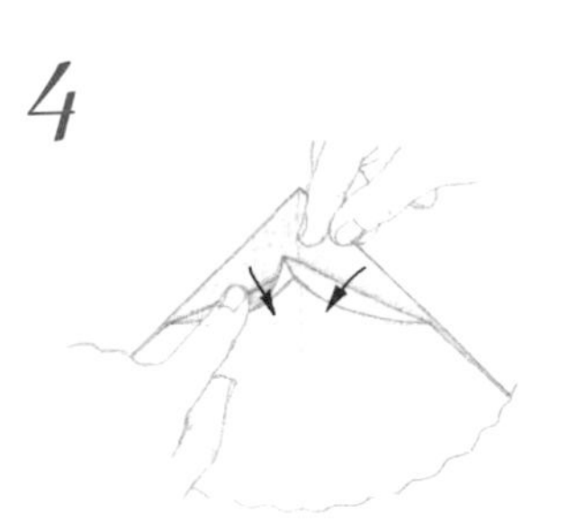

Pinch the point's sloping edges together along the fold-lines made in step 3. Valley fold the small triangular flap that appears to the left, to make the rooster's comb.

5

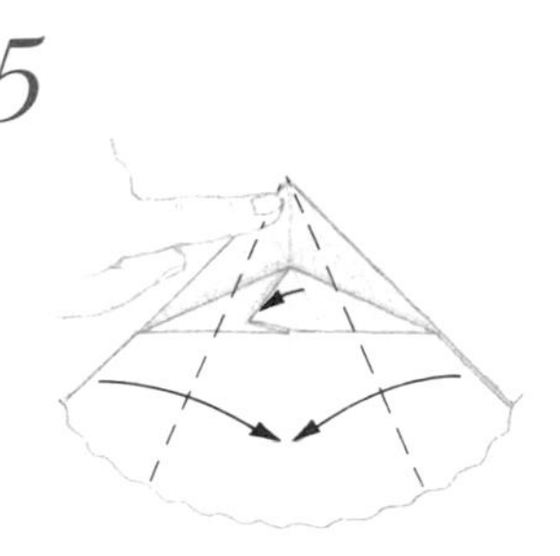

From the top point, valley fold the sloping edges in to meet the middle fold-line. The rooster's comb should remain visible.

6

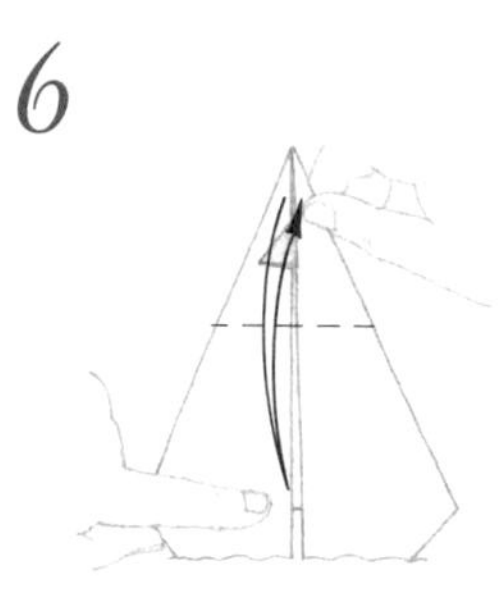

Fold and unfold the top point down to meet the horizontal edge that is currently hidden at the back of the model.

10

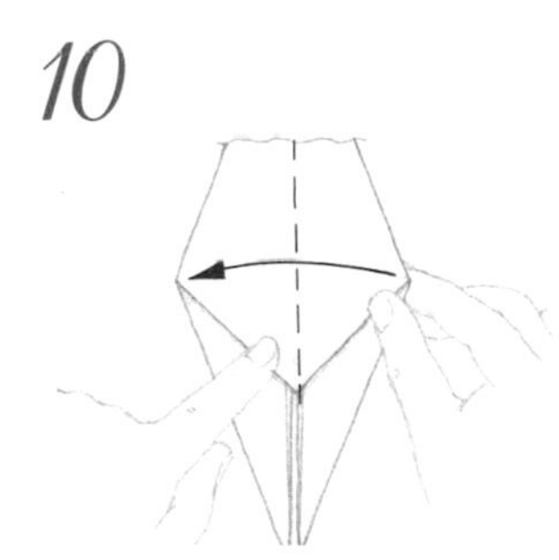

Valley fold the paper in half from right to left.

11

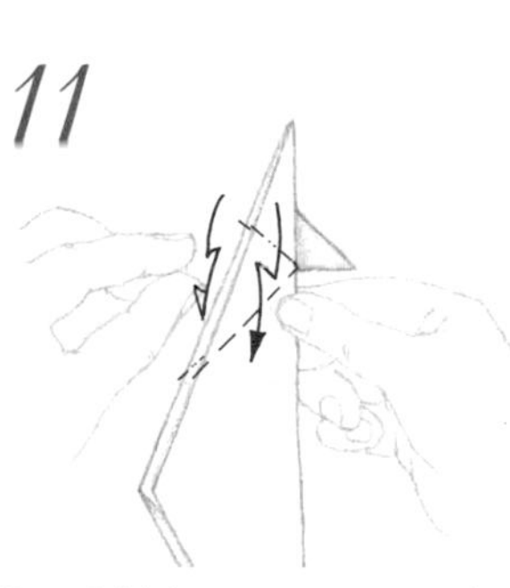

Step fold the top point on either side, as shown, to make the rooster's head.

12

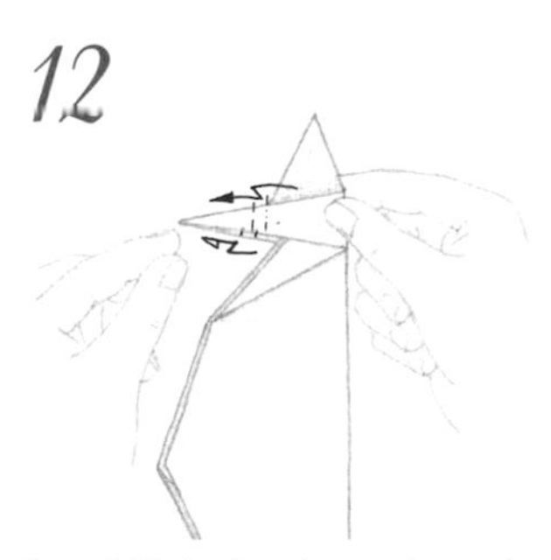

Step fold the head on either side as shown, to make the beak.

13

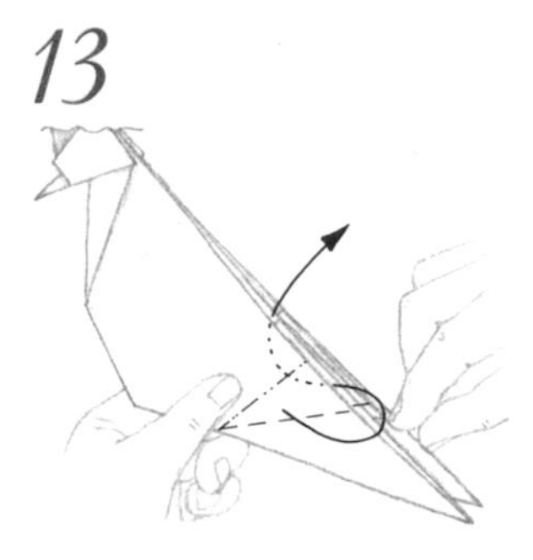

Inside reverse fold a bottom point upwards, while at the same time opening it out into the position shown in step 14.

14

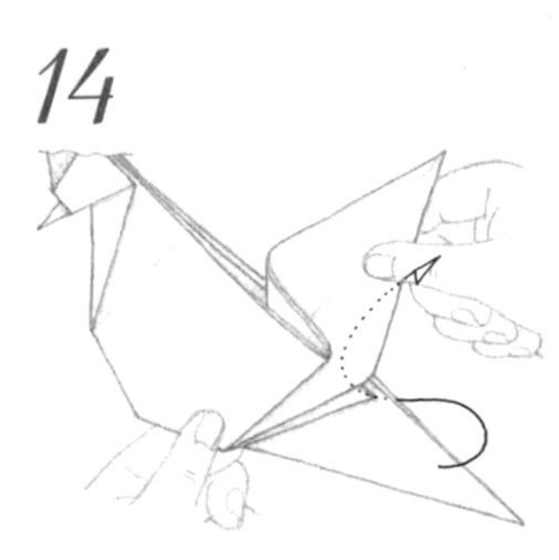

Repeat step 13 with the other bottom point, to produce tail feathers.

15

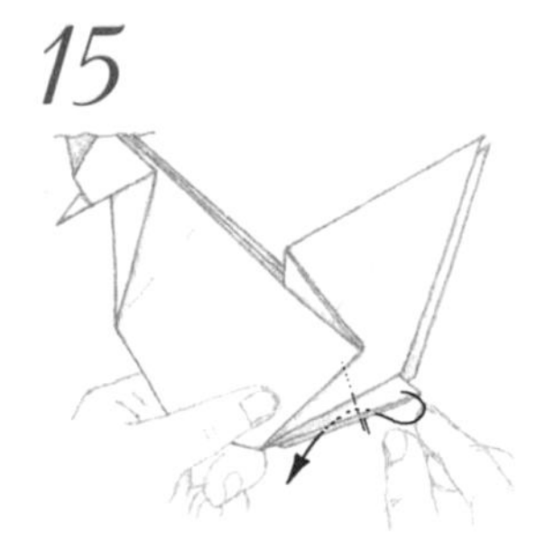

Inside reverse fold the triangular flap to the left, to make the feet.

16

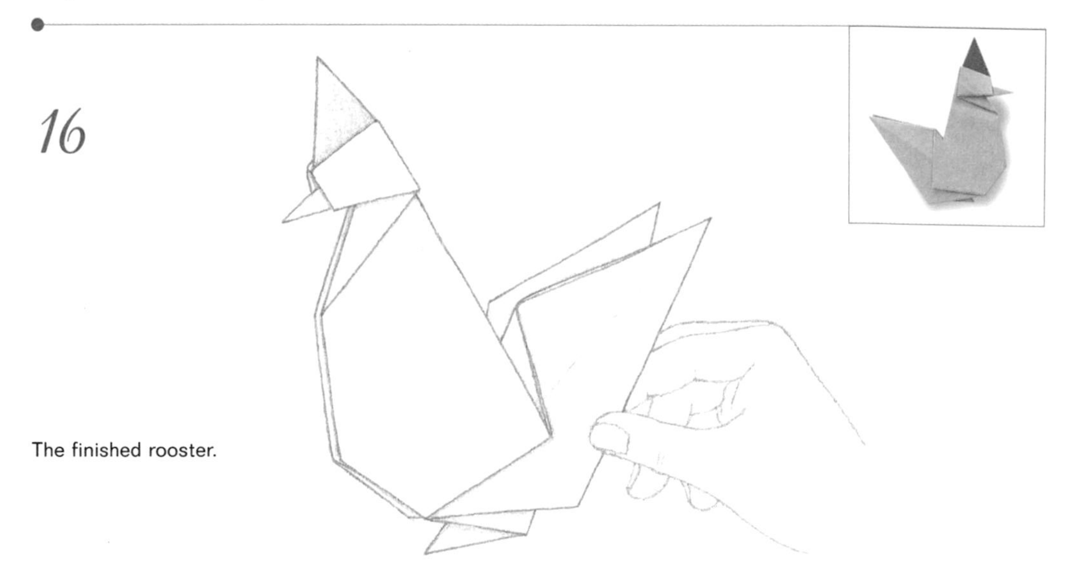

The finished rooster.

Dog

Making Your Dog

Many types of dog can evolve from the diamond base. Try experimenting with folding techniques that are similar to each other, such as step folds and reverse folds, to invent your own origami dog. Use a square piece of paper, white side up.

1

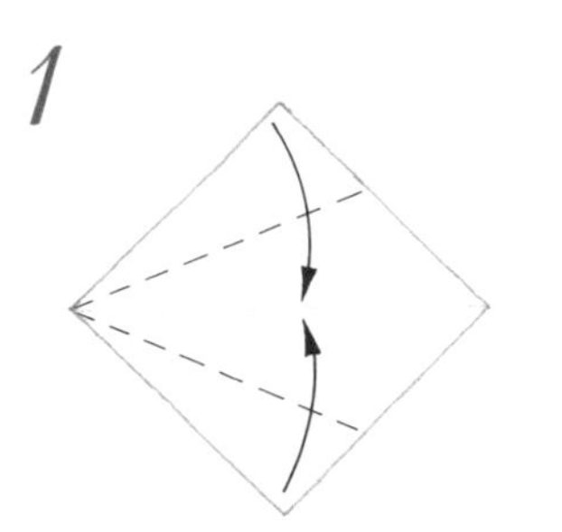

Crease the middle fold-line as shown. From the left-hand point, valley fold the edges in to meet the fold-line, making a kite base.

2

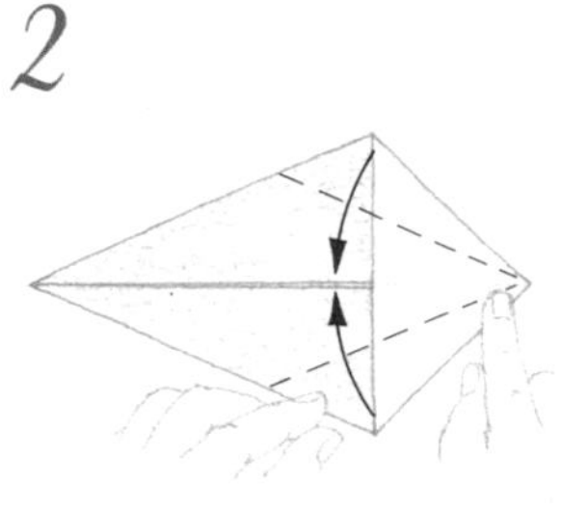

From the right-hand point, valley fold the sloping edges in to meet the middle fold-line, to make a diamond base.

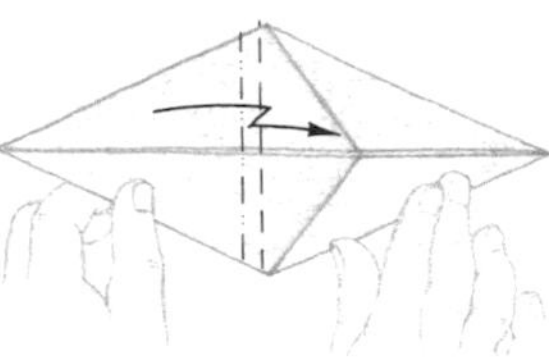

Step fold the left-hand point as shown.

7

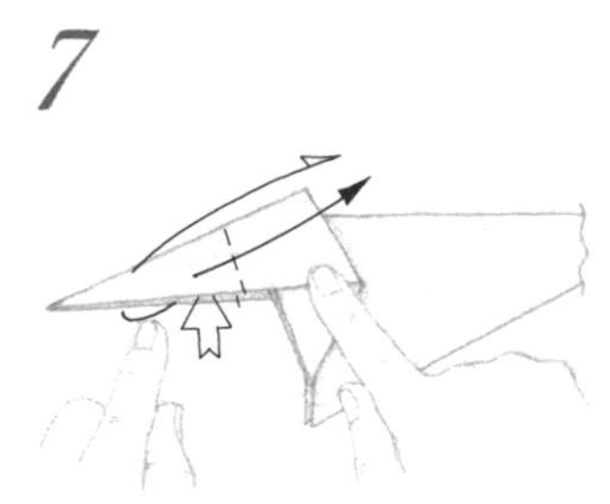

Once again, outside reverse fold the point, to make the dog's head.

8

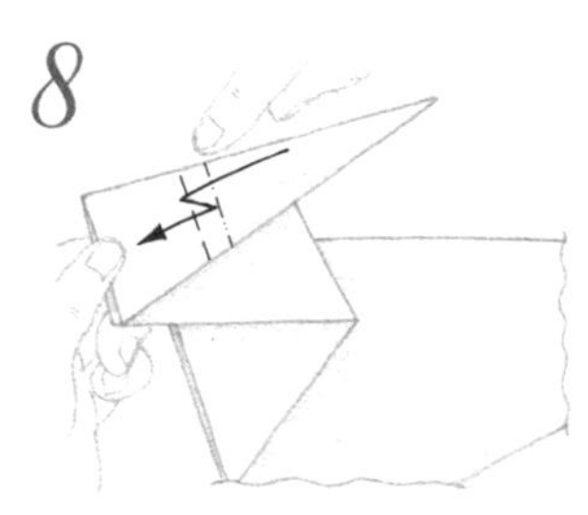

Step fold the head on either side as shown.

9

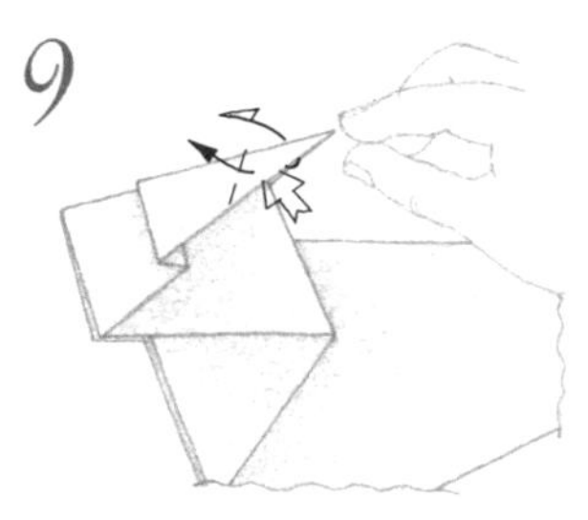

Outside reverse fold the head's tip, to suggest the dog's ears.

4

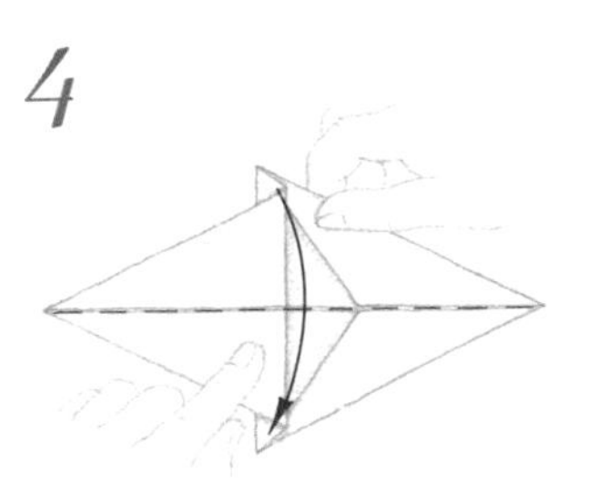

Valley fold the paper in half from top to bottom.

5

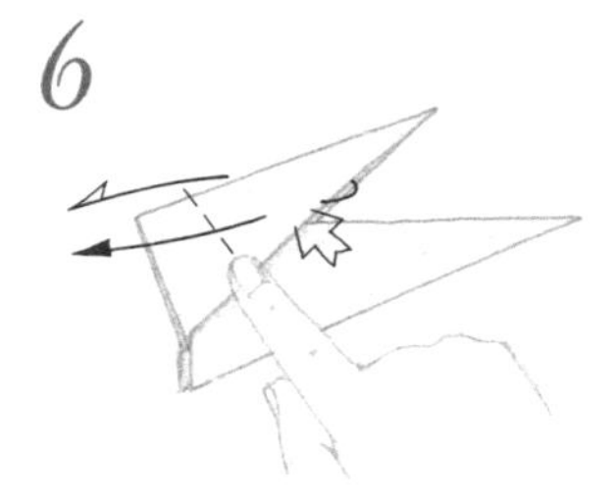

Outside reverse fold the left-hand point into the position shown in step 6.

6

Again, outside reverse fold the point, so it points to the left.

10

Shape the head with a mountain fold. Repeat behind.

11

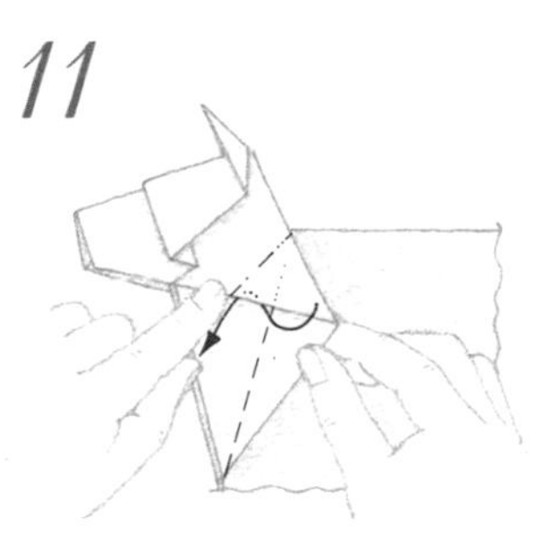

Valley fold the neck's top layer in half, while pushing the triangular area inwards as shown by the mountain fold-line. Repeat behind.

12

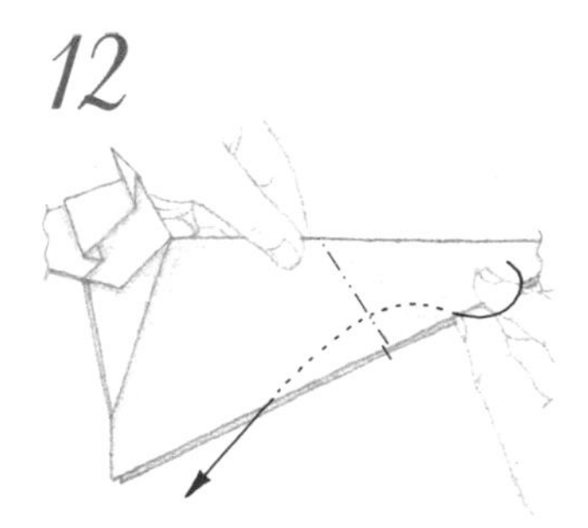

Inside reverse fold the right-hand point into the position shown in step 13.

13

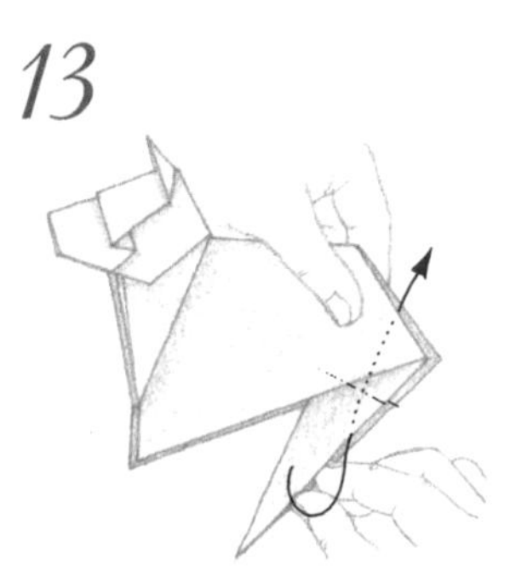

Reverse fold the point back out again, to make the dog's hind legs and tail.

14

On a line from the base of the tail to the step fold, mountain fold the bottom edges while narrowing the hind legs with a valley fold.

15

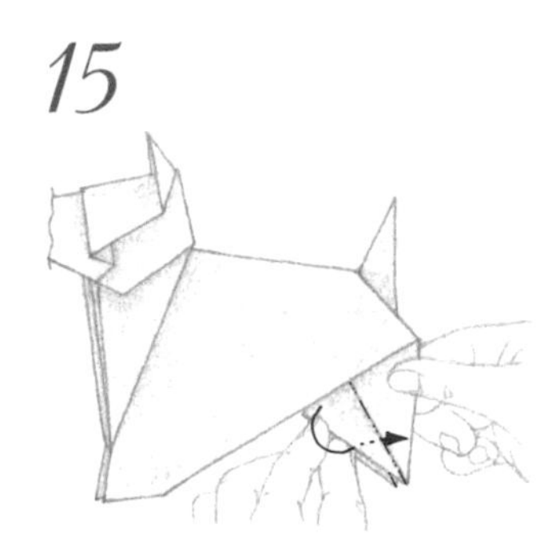

Inside reverse fold the triangular section of paper between the hind legs, as shown, to separate them slightly.

16

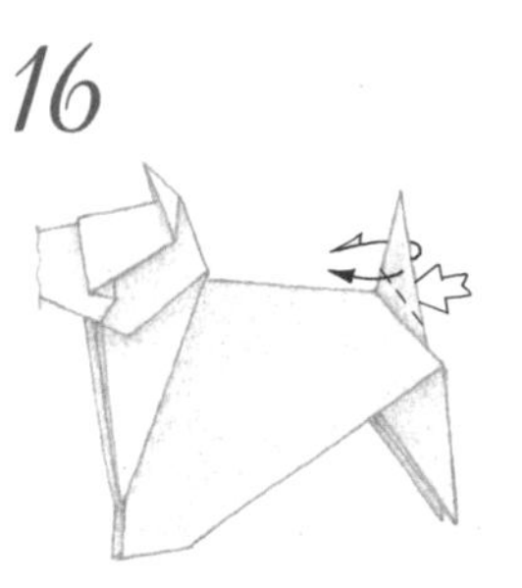

Outside reverse fold the tail's tip.

17

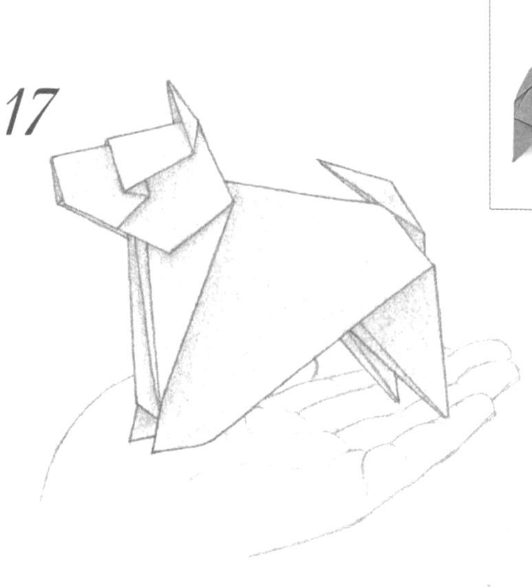

The completed dog.

Pig

Making Your Pig

If you use a few folds to form just main features, you can create a model that is simple yet clearly resembles a particular object. This pig is a perfect example of that technique. Use a square piece of paper, white side up.

1

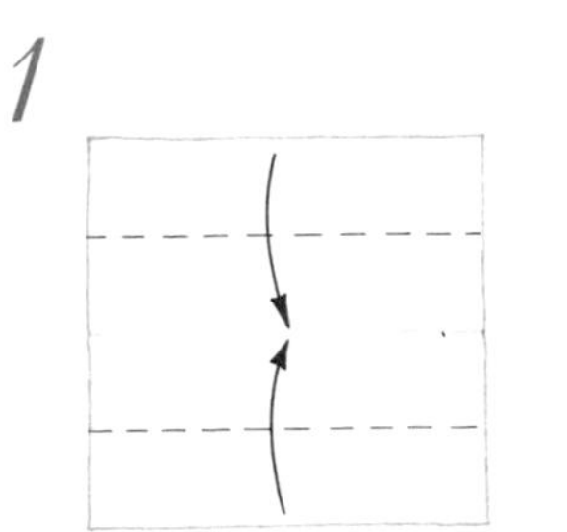

Crease the middle fold-line as shown. Valley fold the top and bottom edges to meet the middle fold-line.

2

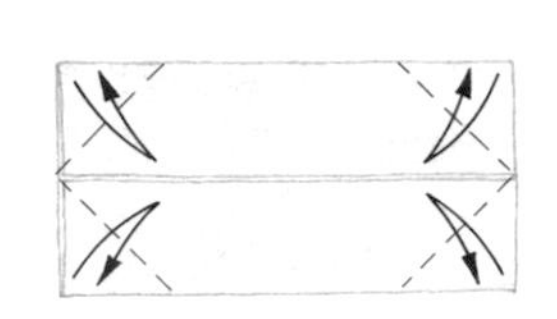

Fold and unfold the corners as shown.

3

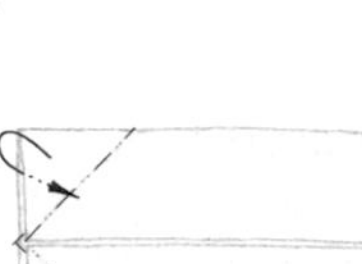

Inside reverse fold the corners along the fold-lines made in step 2, to make four points.

7

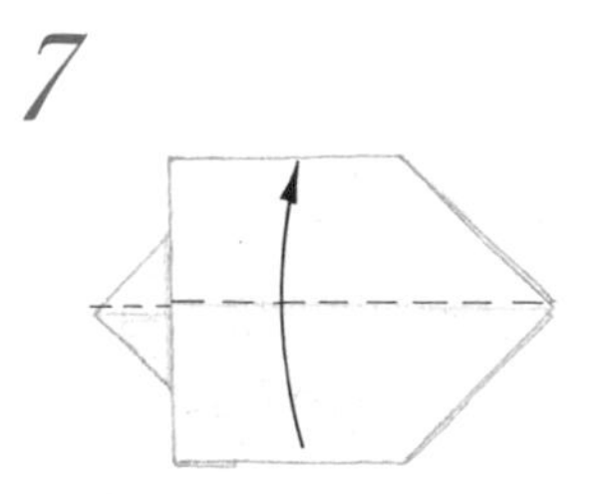

Valley fold the paper in half from bottom to top.

8

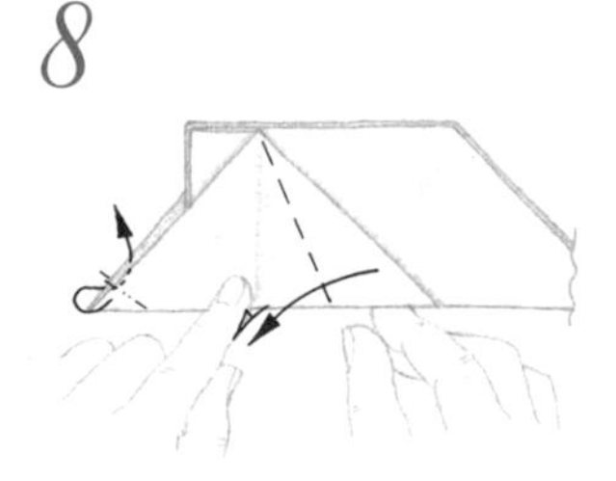

Inside reverse fold the left-hand point making the snout. Valley fold the triangle to make a front leg, as shown in step 9. Repeat behind.

9

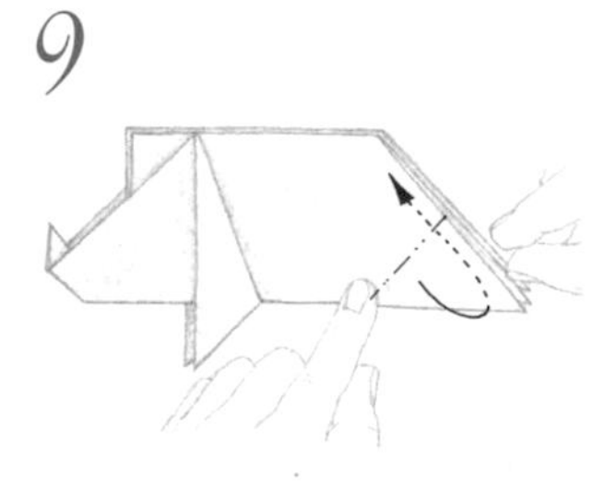

Taking the top layer only, mountain fold the bottom right-hand point up ...

4

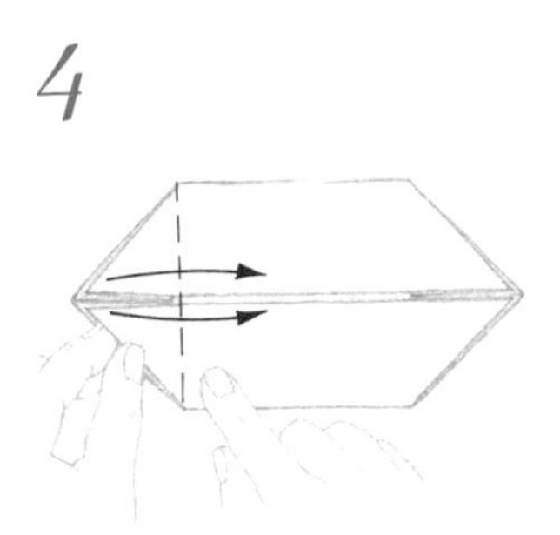

Valley fold the two left-hand points over to the right, revealing a triangle shape underneath.

5

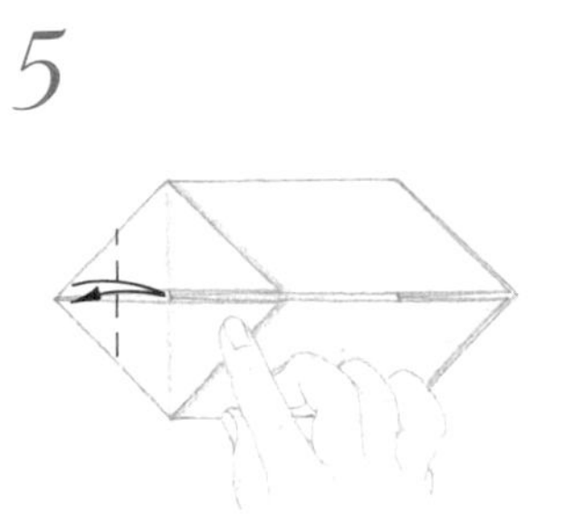

Fold and unfold this triangle, as shown.

6

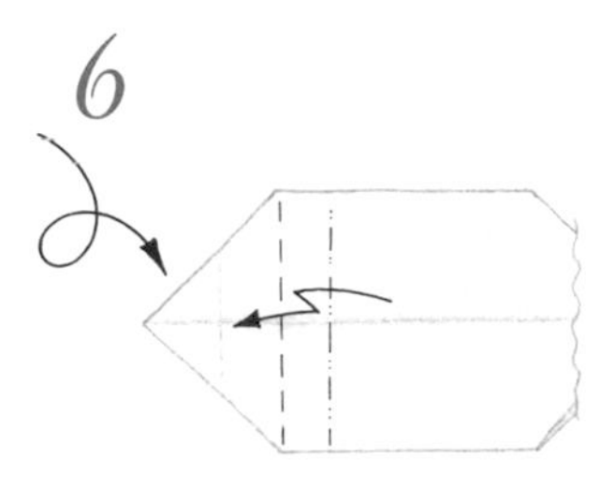

Turn the paper over. Step fold the left-hand section using the fold-line from step 5 as a guide. Don't fold the flaps that are underneath.

10

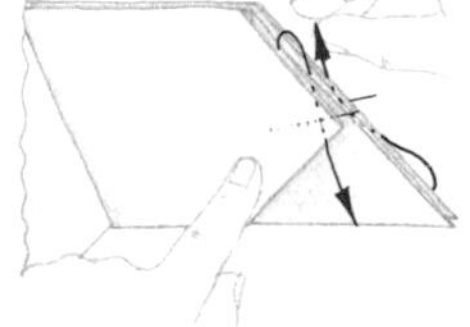

... and back down into the position shown in step 11. Turn the pig over and repeat steps 9 and 10. This makes the back legs.

11

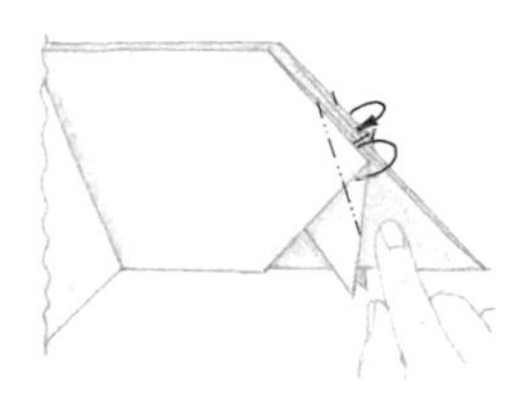

Shape the back legs with a mountain fold on each side.

12

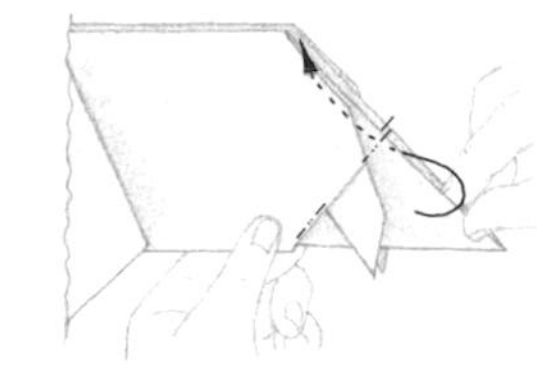

Inside reverse fold the remaining right-hand point up inside the model, to make the tail.

13

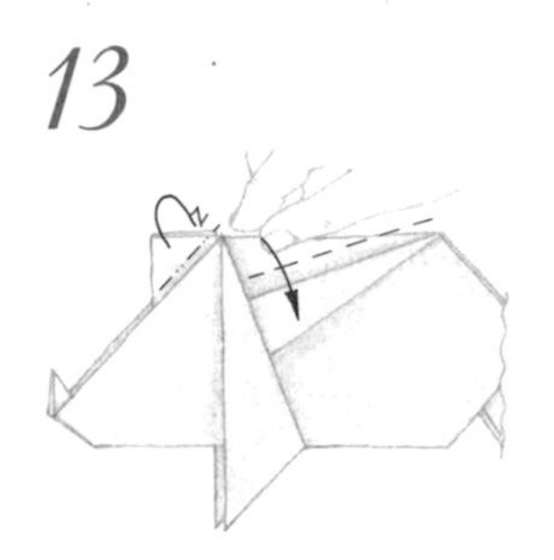

Shape the pig's back with a valley fold as shown, while at the same time squashing down the adjoining point.

14

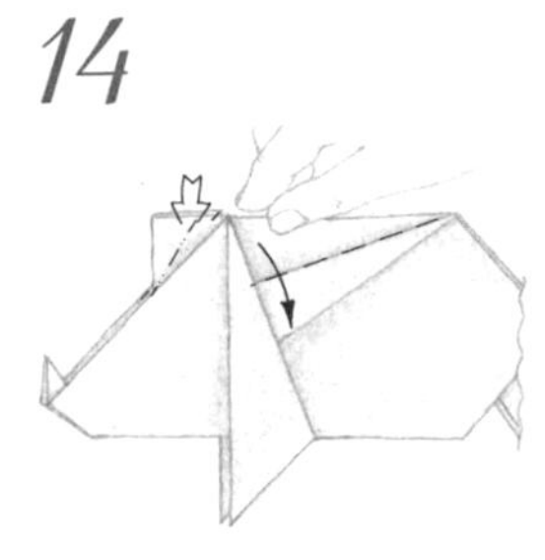

Repeat step 13 with the remaining flap, but valley fold over the previous fold as shown, to close up the pig's back.

15

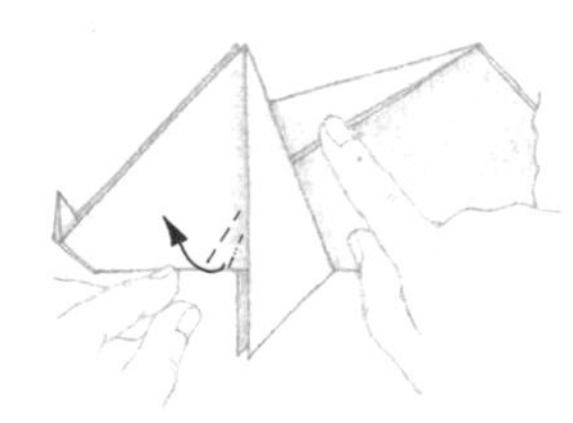

Release a little of the paper adjacent to the front leg and step fold it as shown, to suggest a tusk. Repeat behind.

16

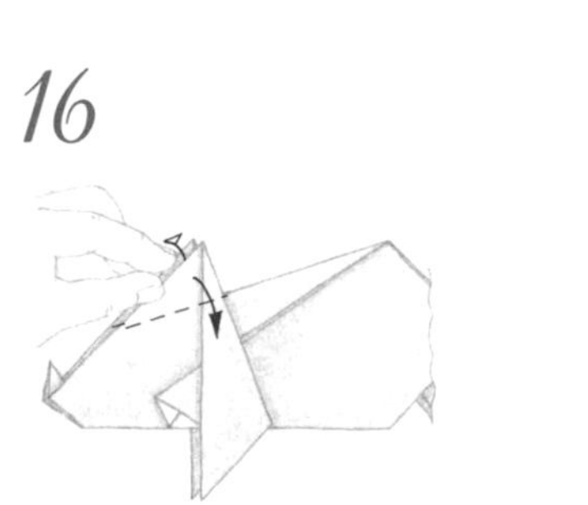

Valley fold the two top points down slightly to make the ears.

17

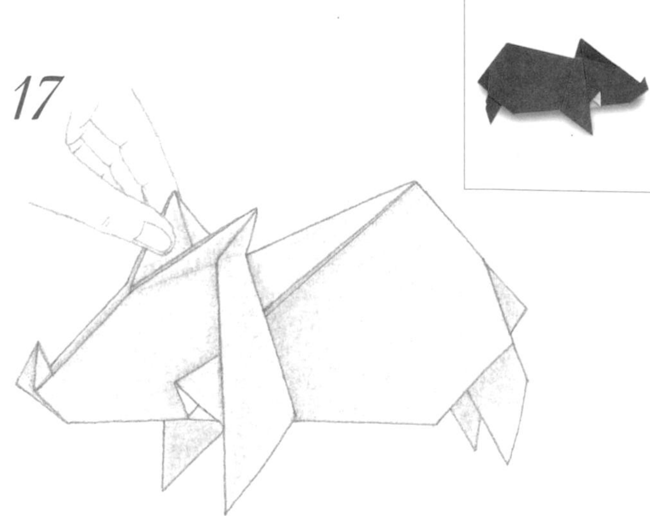

Your pig is finished.

Rat

Making Your Rat

To enhance the finished result, try to use paper that matches a rat's appearance. Use a square piece of paper, coloured side up.

1

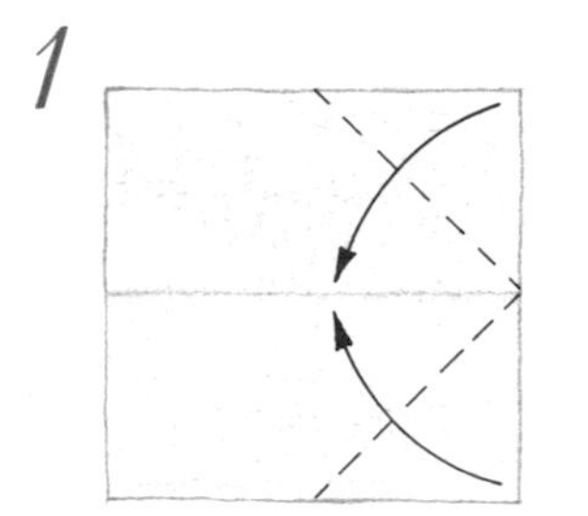

Crease the middle fold-line as shown. Valley fold the right-hand corners in to meet the middle fold-line.

2

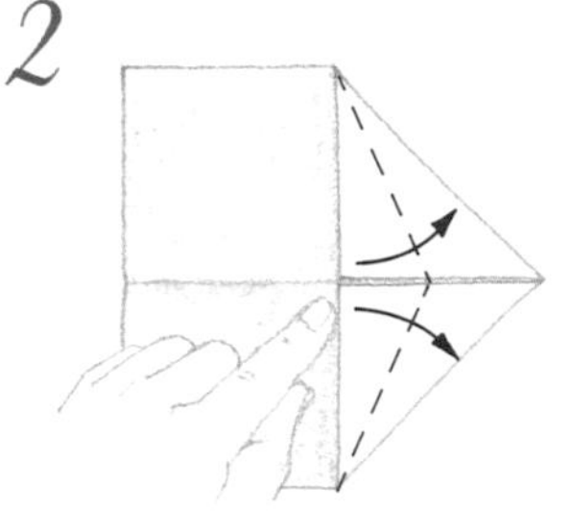

Valley fold the corners as shown.

3

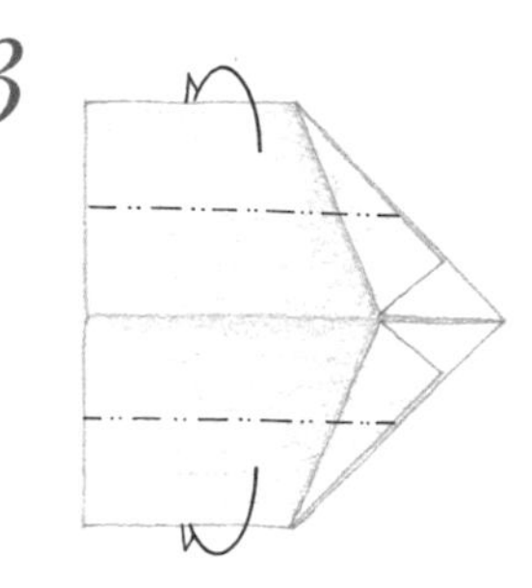

Mountain fold the top and bottom edges to meet the middle fold-line.

7

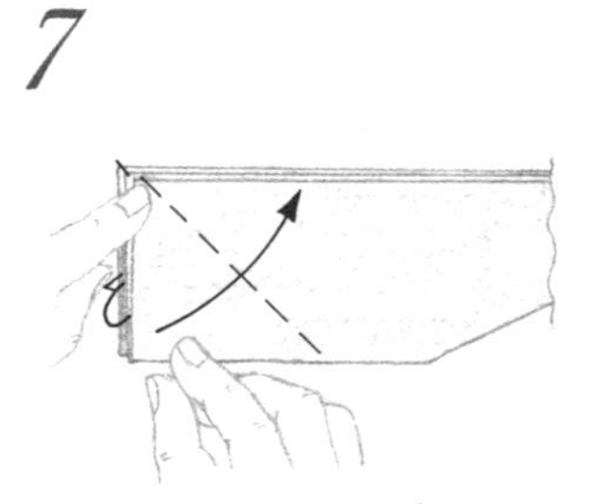

Valley fold the bottom left-hand corner (top layer only) up to meet the top edge. Repeat behind.

8

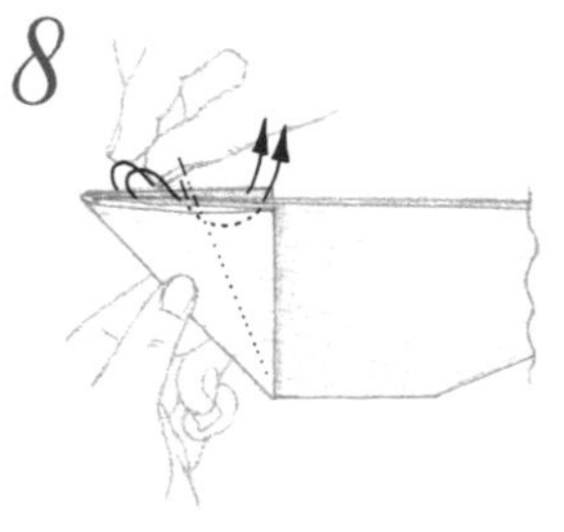

Inside reverse fold the hidden point upwards, to make an ear. Repeat behind.

9

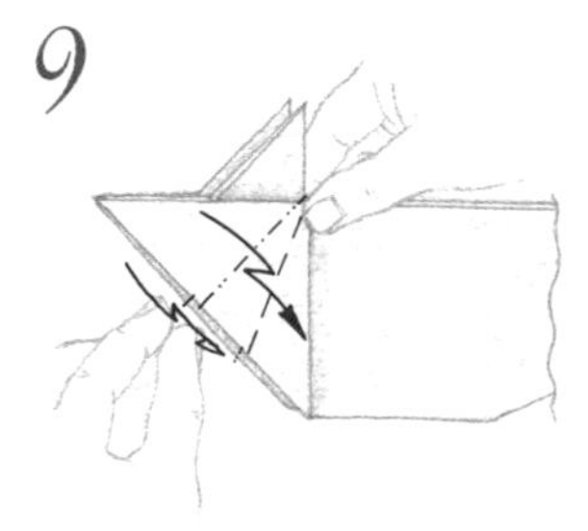

Step fold the left-hand point on either side as shown, to make the head.

4

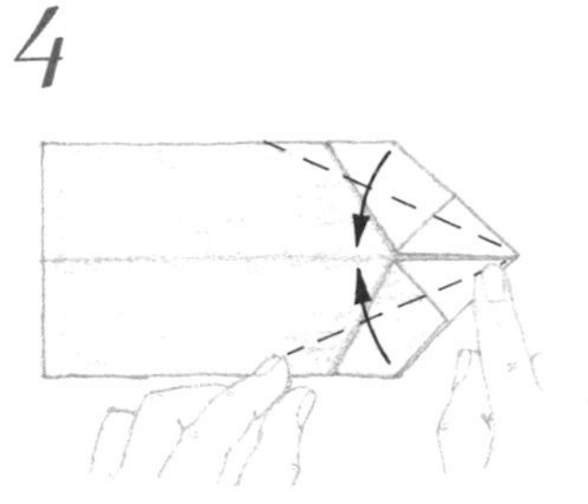

From the right-hand point, valley fold the sloping edges in to meet the middle fold-line.

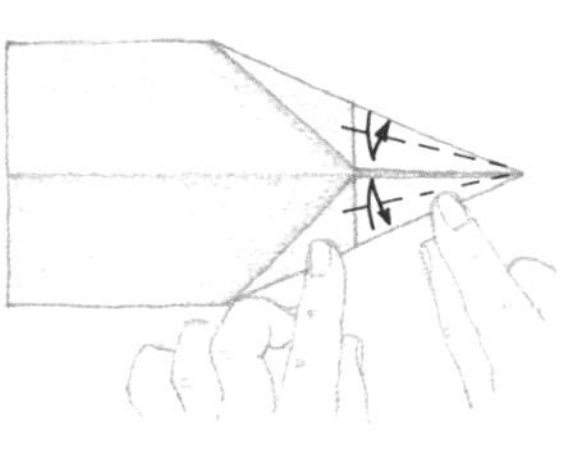

Again from the right-hand point, fold and unfold the sloping edges in to the middle fold-line. Crease them only as far as shown.

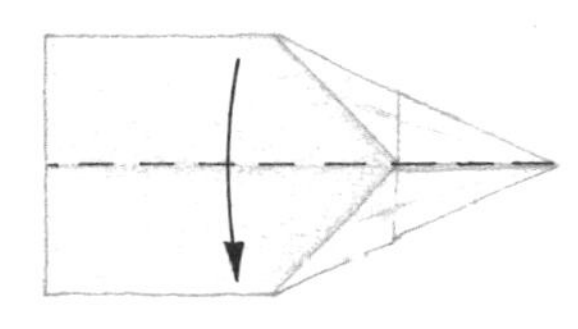

Valley fold the paper in half from top to bottom.

10

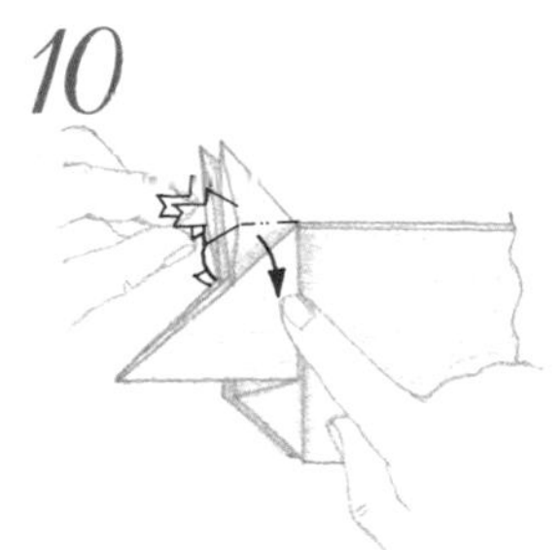

Open out an ear and squash it down neatly. Repeat with the other ear.

11

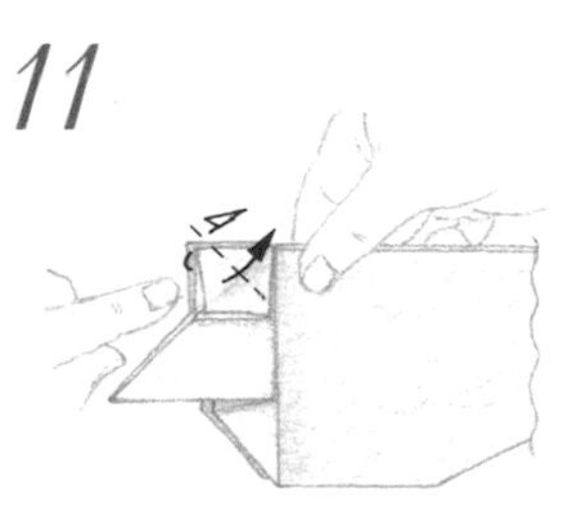

Then open the ears out to make them three-dimensional.

12

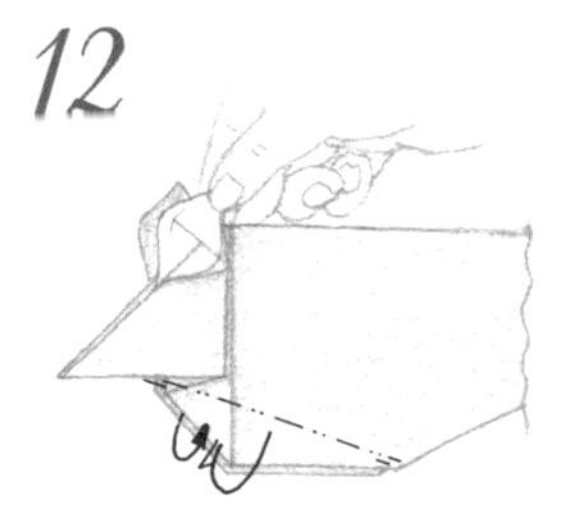

Shape the rat's underside with a mountain fold on each side.

13

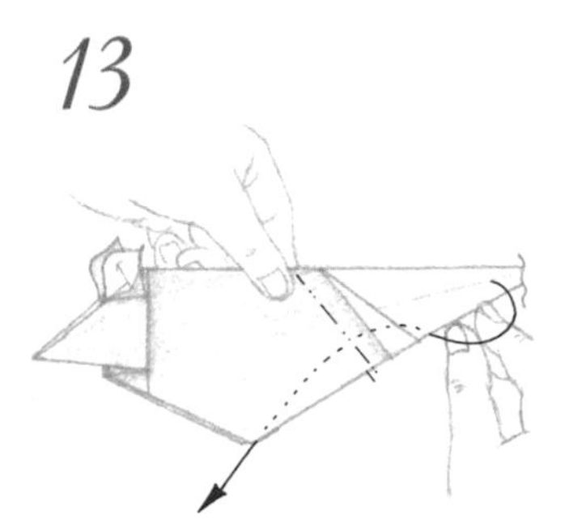

Inside reverse fold the right-hand point down inside the model and ...

14

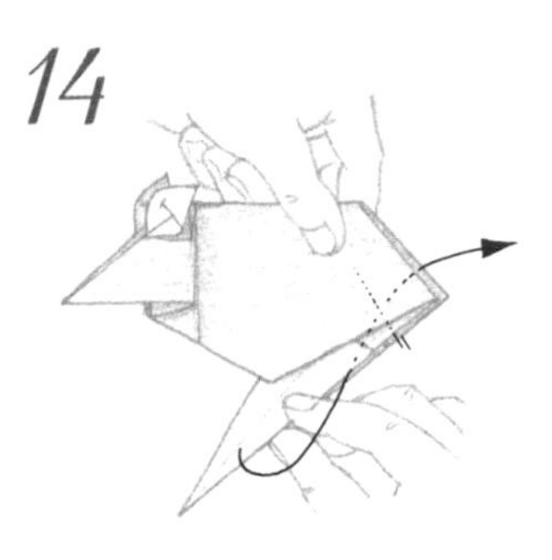

... back out as shown, to make the tail.

15

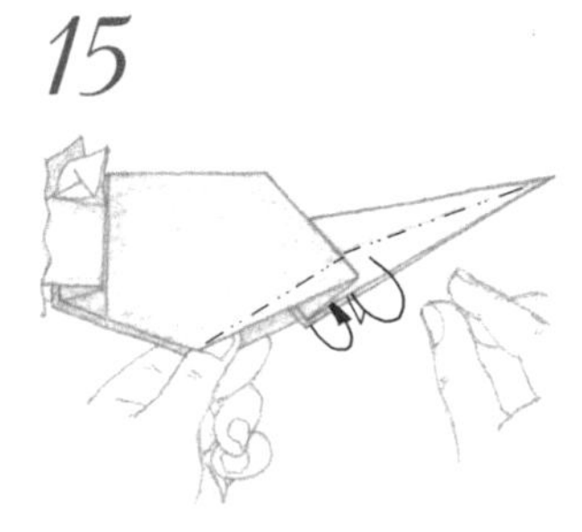

Narrow down the tail with a mountain fold on each side. These folds take place along the fold-lines made in step 5.

16

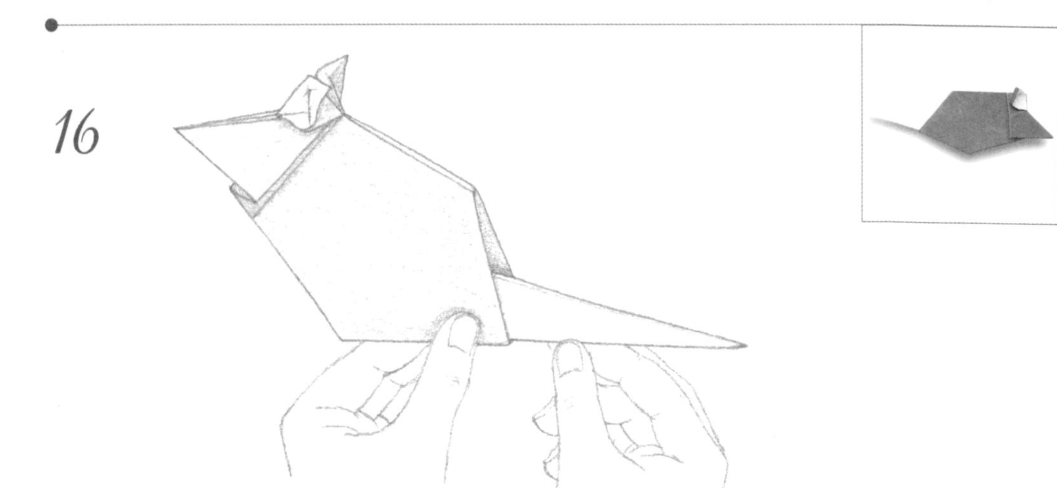

The completed rat.

Ox

Making Your Ox

The folds in steps 6, 7 and 11 can prove tricky, but with a little patience they will fall into place. Use a square piece of paper, white side up.

1

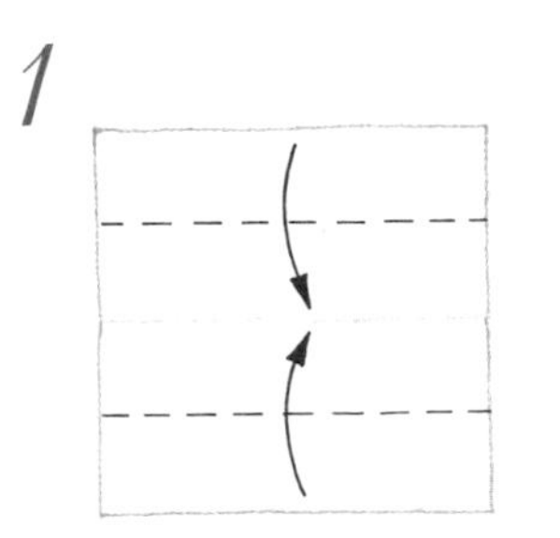

Crease the middle fold-line as shown. Valley fold the top and bottom edges in to meet the middle fold-line.

2

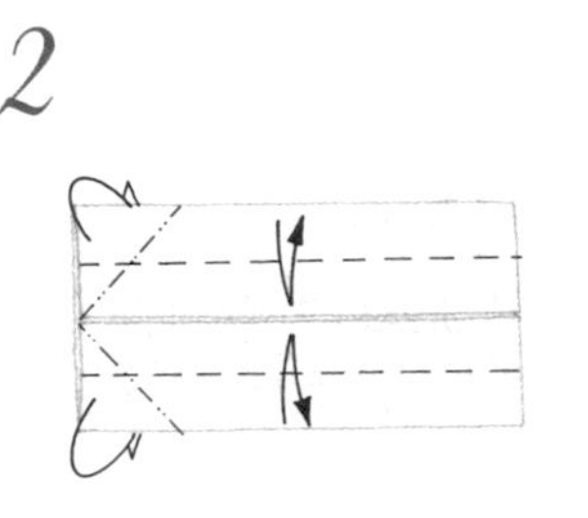

Fold and unfold the top and bottom edges. Mountain fold the left-hand corners behind to meet the middle fold-line.

3

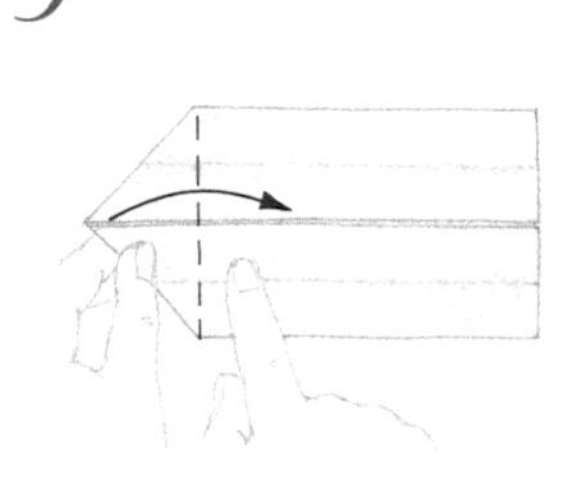

Valley fold the left-hand point.

7

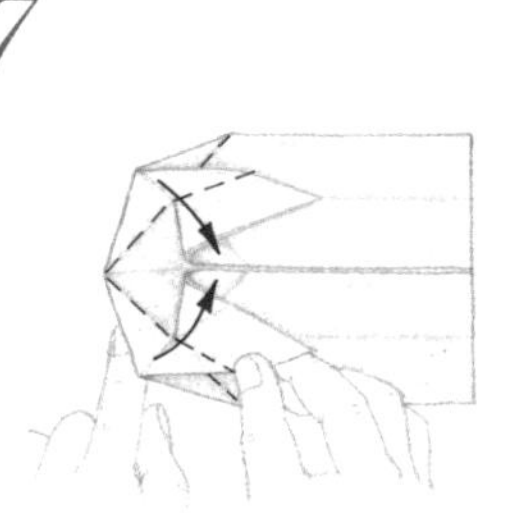

... and fold the flaps along the middle fold-line, as shown in step 8. This makes the ox's horns.

8

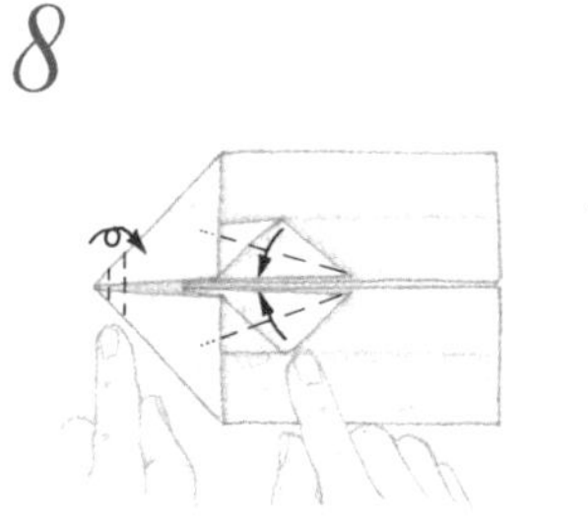

Valley fold each horn in half. Fold over and over a little of the left-hand point twice, to make the ox's snout.

9

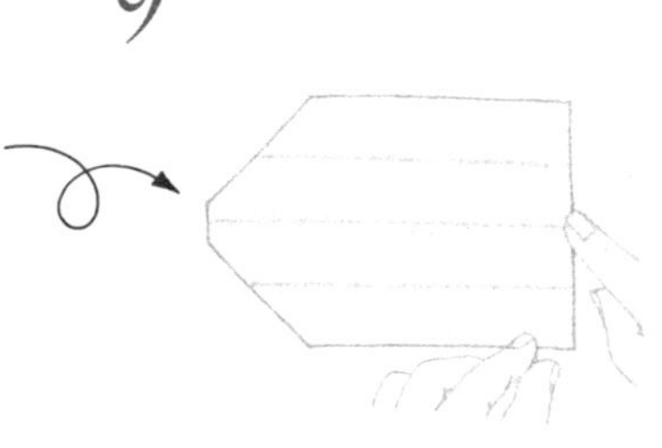

Turn the paper over. Step fold the left-hand section as shown. Valley fold both right-hand corners to meet their adjacent fold-lines, so they form a point.

4

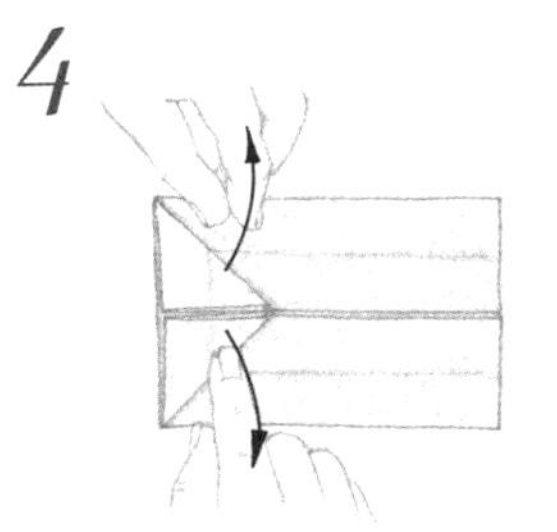

Pinch the point's outer layers and pull them apart, into the position shown in step 5. Press them flat to make two triangular flaps.

5

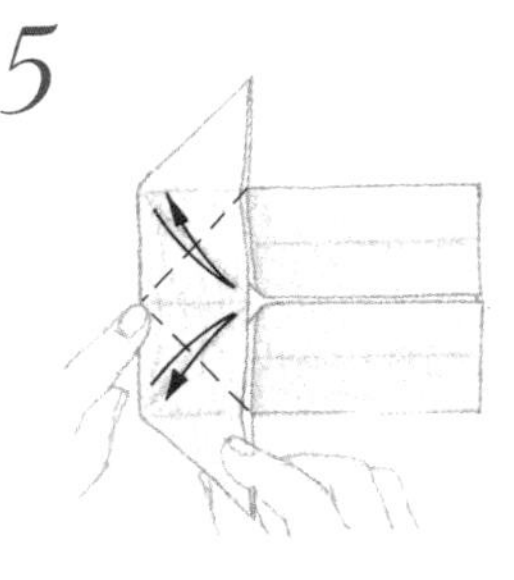

Fold and unfold the flaps as shown.

6

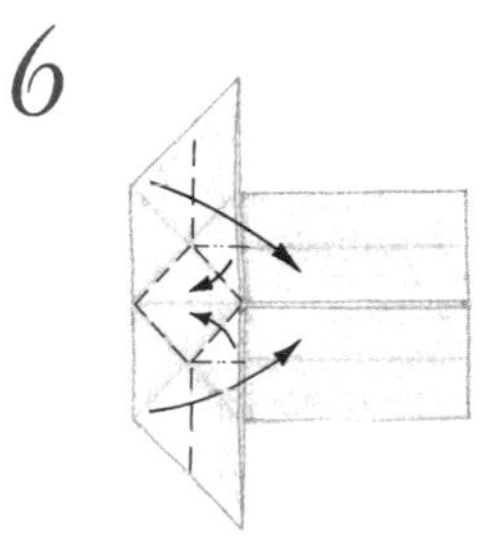

Carefully fold the flaps along the creases made in the previous step, while folding the two middle triangles up into the diamond …

10

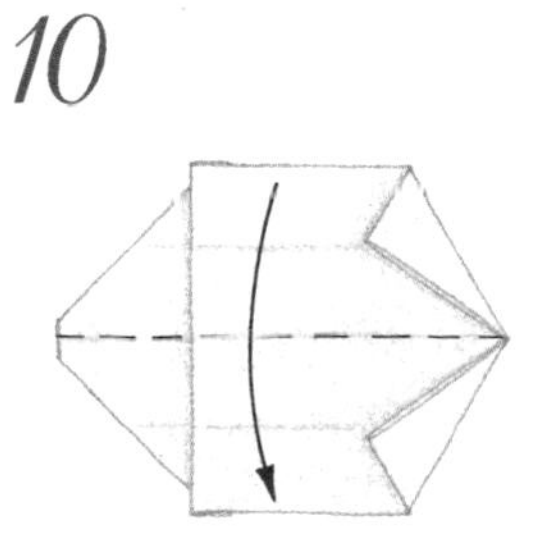

Valley fold the paper in half from top to bottom.

11

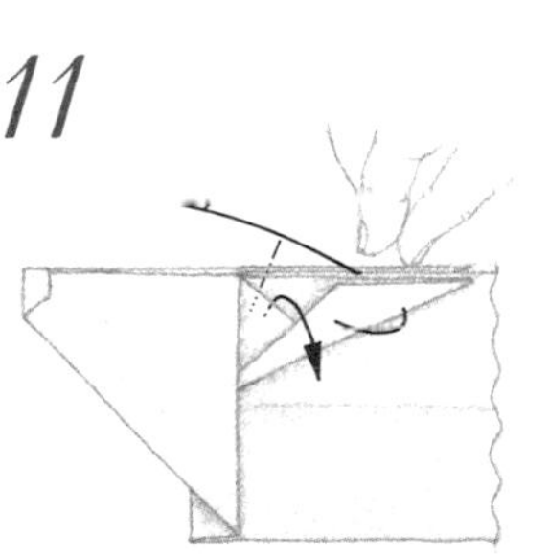

Mountain fold a horn upwards, and at the same time release the triangular section from inside the horn, as shown, to make an ear. Repeat behind.

12

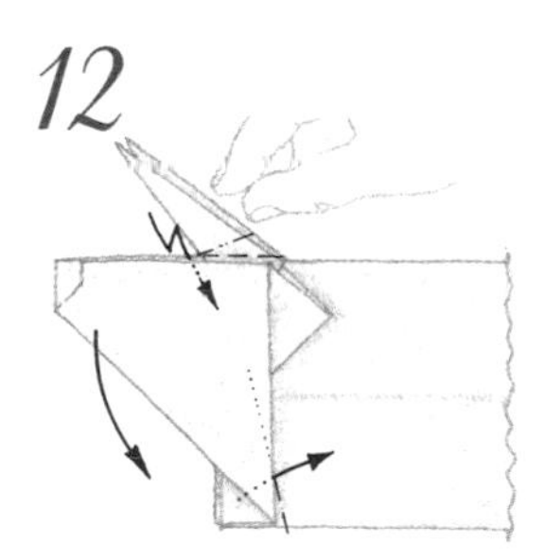

Step fold the horns down inside the model. Pull the snout downwards slightly. Press it flat, into the position shown in step 13. This makes the ox's head.

13

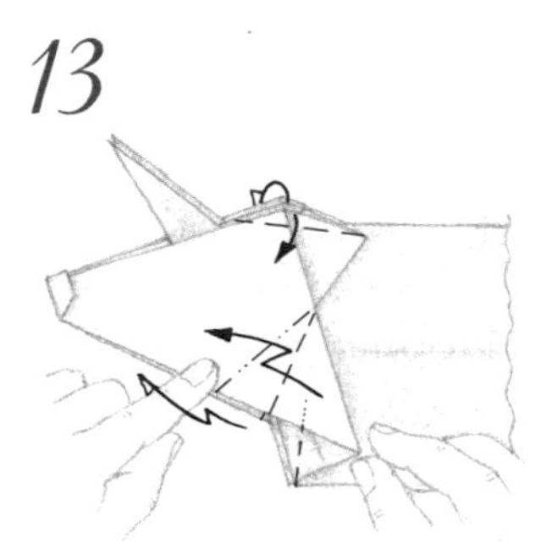

Valley fold the head's top point slightly. Repeat behind. Step fold the neck into place on either side, as shown.

14

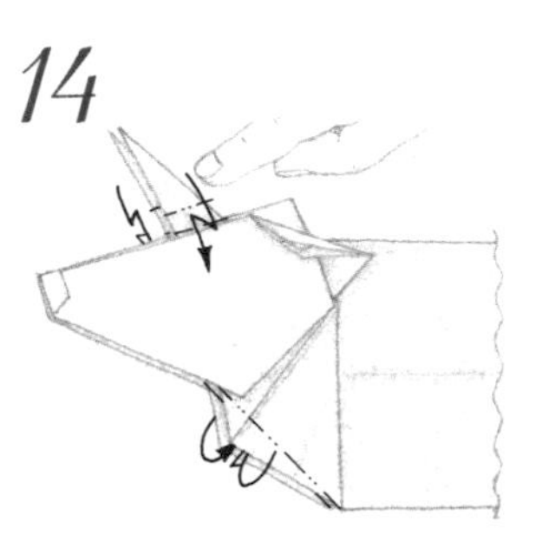

Shape a horn with a step fold. Mountain fold a little of the neck inside the model. Repeat both procedures behind.

15

Inside reverse fold a little of the right-hand point downwards, to make the ox's tail.

16

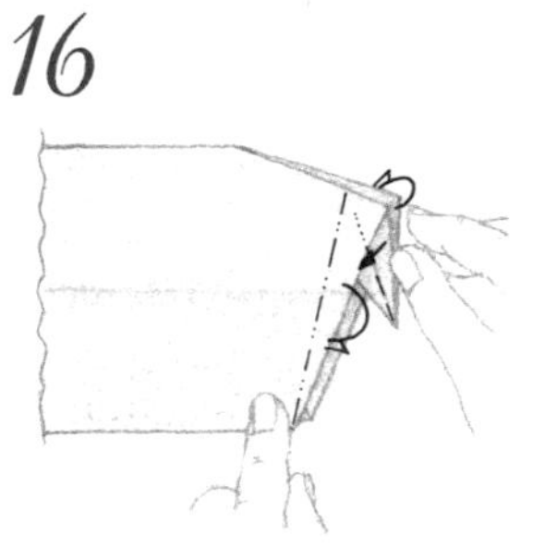

Valley fold the tail's top layer in half, while at the same time pushing the triangular area inwards as shown by the mountain fold-line. Repeat behind.

17

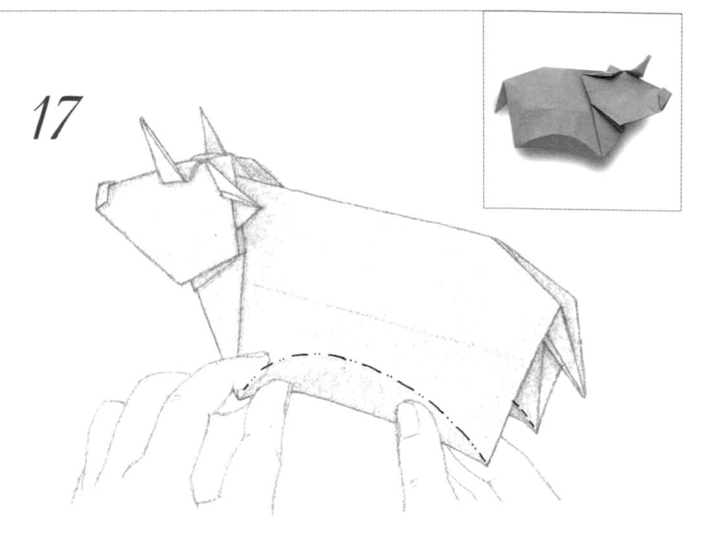

To complete the ox, mountain fold the bottom edges inwards slightly.

Rabbit

Making Your Rabbit

In the world of origami, animals can be particularly challenging. Once you have folded an animal, slight variations can be introduced to change its overall shape and form. Use a square piece of paper, white side up.

1

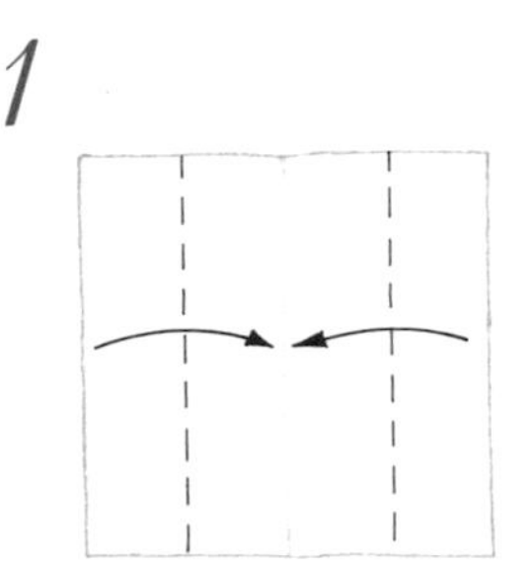

Crease the middle fold-line as shown. Valley fold the sides in to meet the middle fold-line.

2

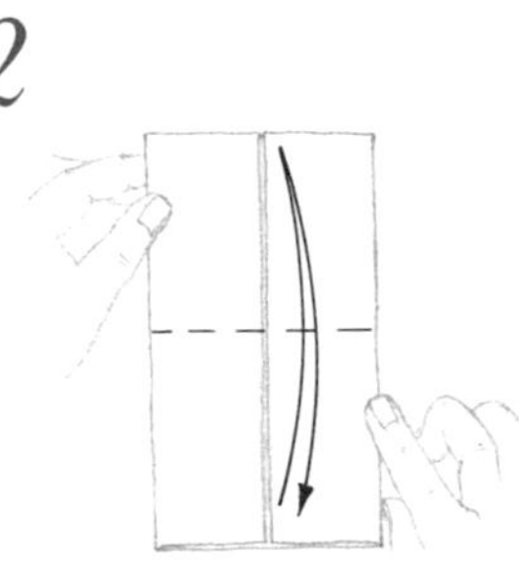

Fold and unfold the paper in half from bottom to top.

3

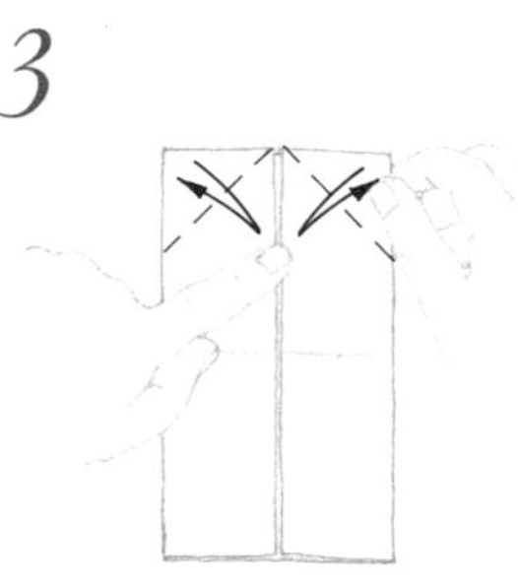

Fold and unfold the top corners as shown.

7

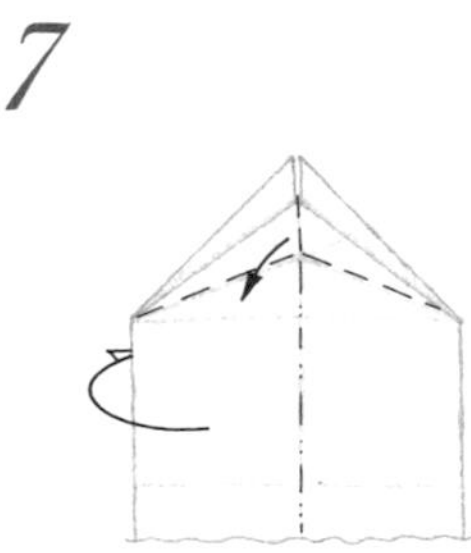

Pinch together the same edges along the fold-lines made in step 6, while mountain folding the paper in half. A flap will appear.

8

Mountain fold the right-hand top layer of paper on a line between the top point and the fold-line made in step 2. Repeat behind.

9

Fold and unfold the paper as shown.

4

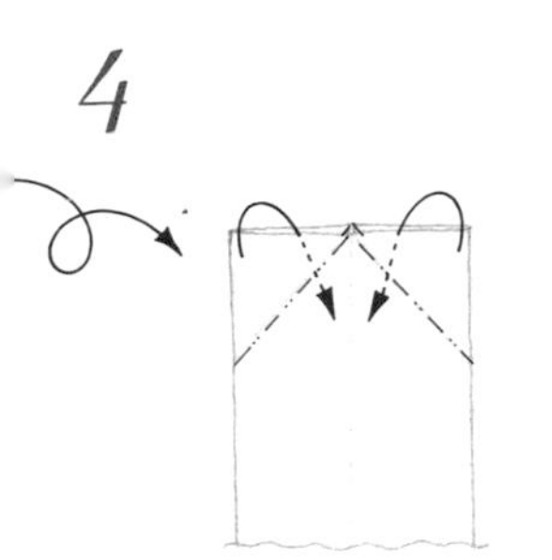

Turn the paper over. Inside reverse fold the corners along the fold-lines made in step 3.

5

Fold and unfold the top point as shown.

6

Fold and unfold the point's sloping edges down to meet the fold-line made in step 5.

10

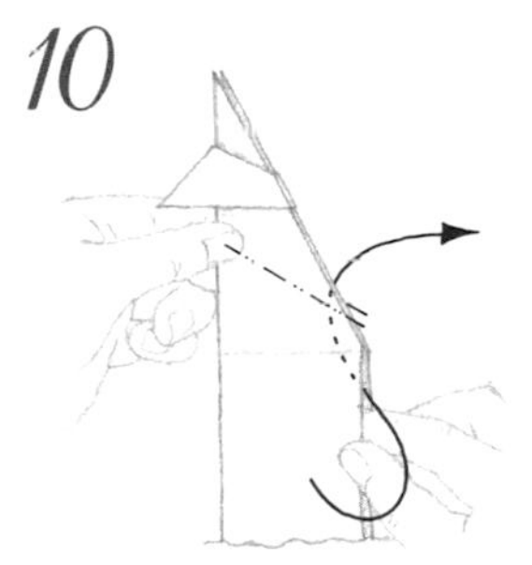

Inside reverse fold the bottom section up to the right along the fold-lines made in step 9.

11

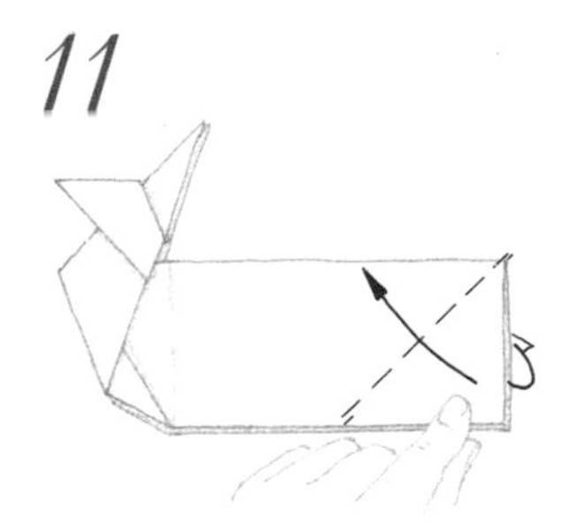

Valley fold the bottom right-hand corner (top layer only) up to meet the top edge. Repeat behind.

12

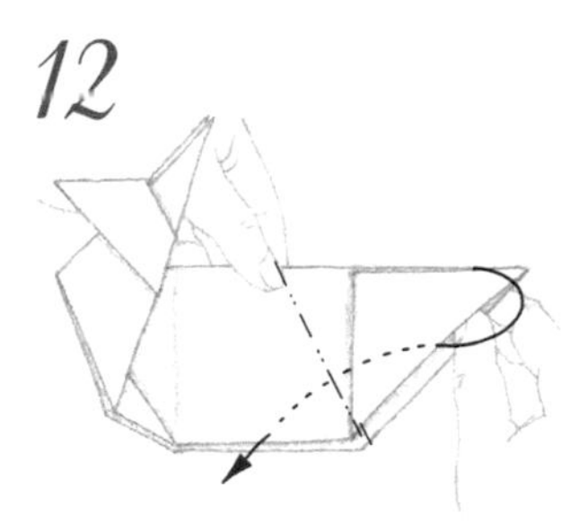

Inside reverse fold the right-hand point into the position shown in step 13.

13

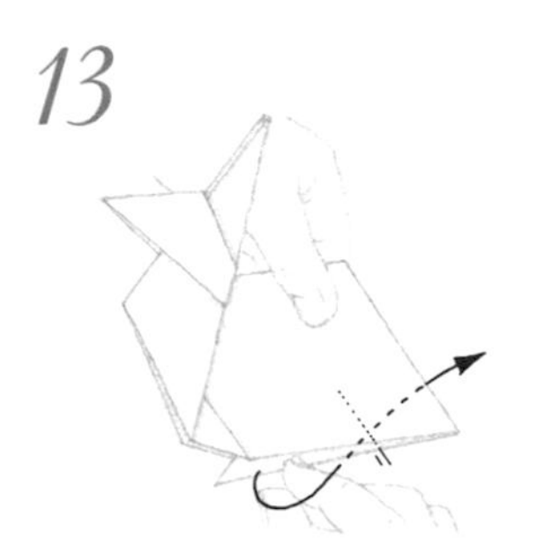

Reverse fold the point back out, to make the rabbit's tail.

14

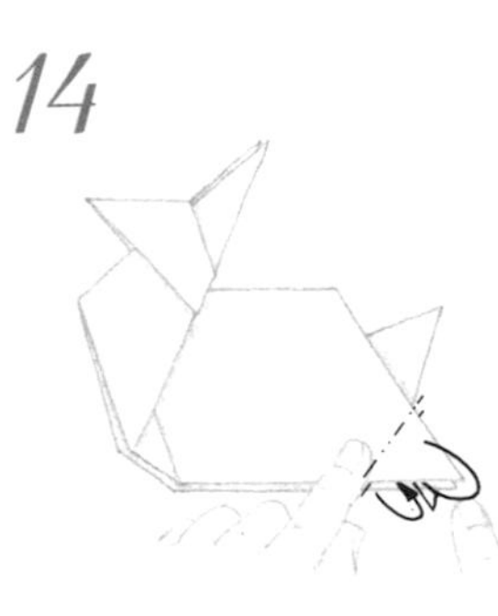

Shape the base of the tail with a mountain fold. Repeat behind.

15

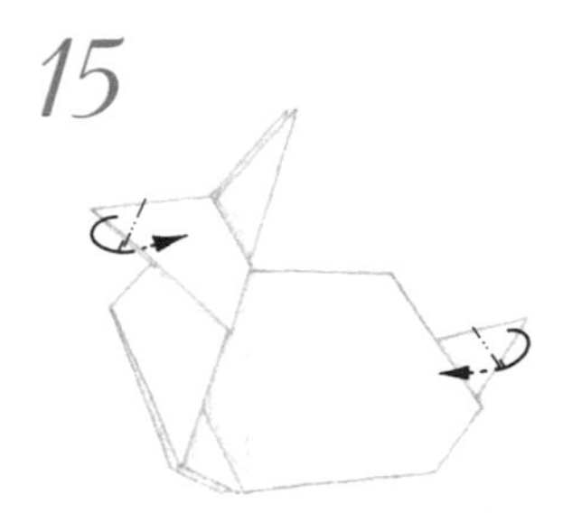

Blunt the rabbit's nose and tail with inside reverse folds.

16

17

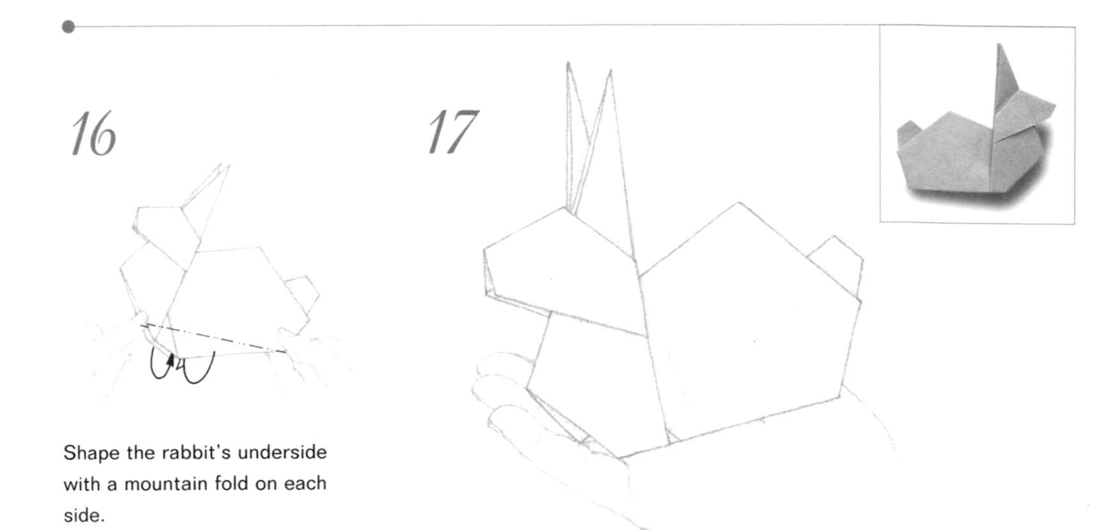

Shape the rabbit's underside with a mountain fold on each side.

The finished rabbit.

Snake

Making Your Snake

The folding of this particular model is based around the reverse fold. It may appear difficult at first but should become easier with practice. Use a square piece of paper, white side up.

1

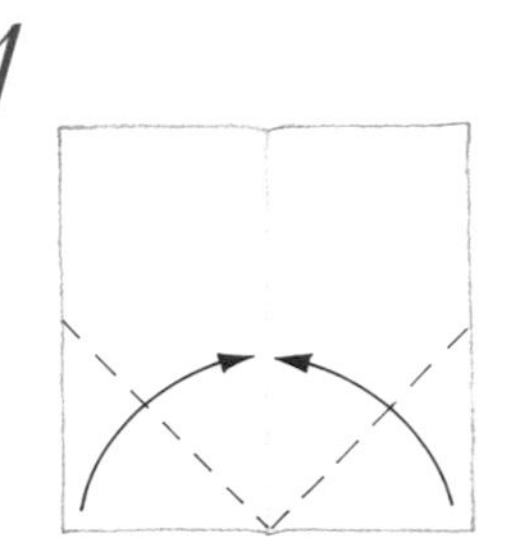

Crease the middle fold-line as shown. Valley fold the bottom corners in to meet the middle fold-line

2

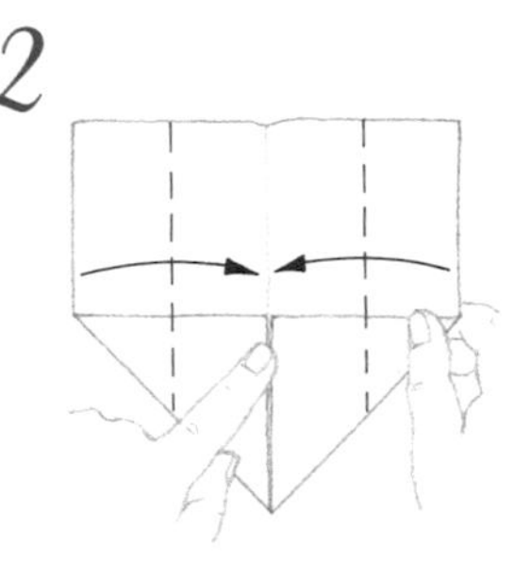

Valley fold the sides in to meet the middle fold-line.

3

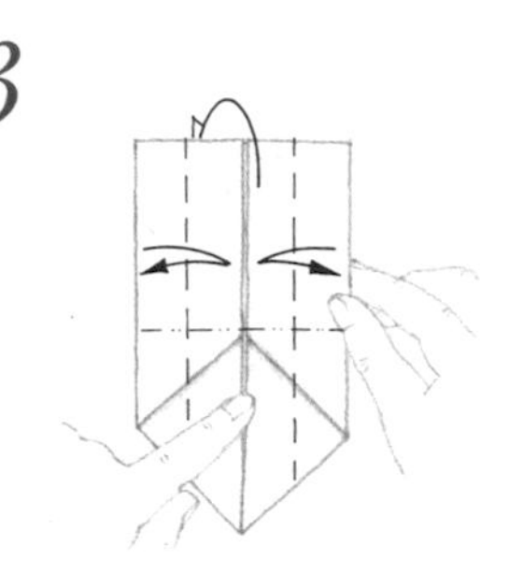

Fold and unfold the sides as shown. Mountain fold the paper in half from top to bottom.

7

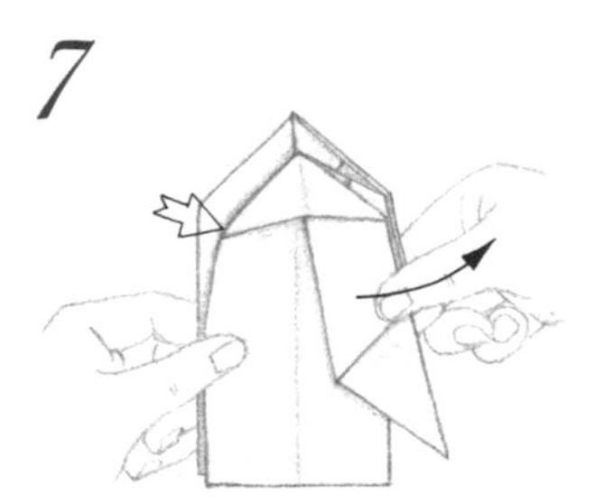

Open out the layers slightly as shown and …

8

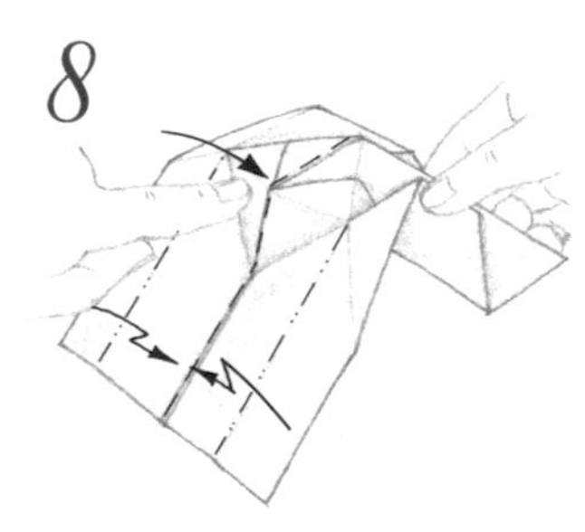

… push the middle ridge down as shown by the valley fold. Mountain fold both sides and flatten them into the position shown in step 9.

9

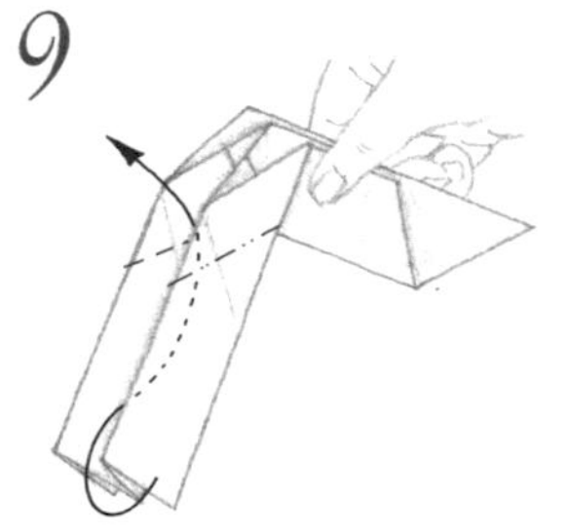

Inside reverse fold the flattened section of paper up and …

4

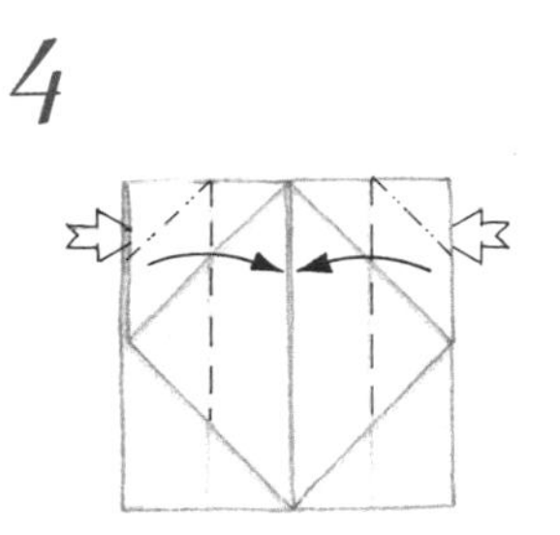

Valley fold the front flap's sides in to meet the middle line and, as you do so …

5

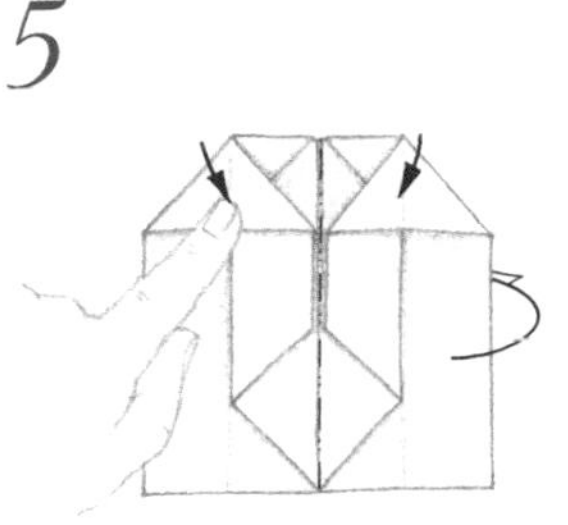

… squash down their top corners into triangles as shown. Mountain fold the paper in half from right to left.

6

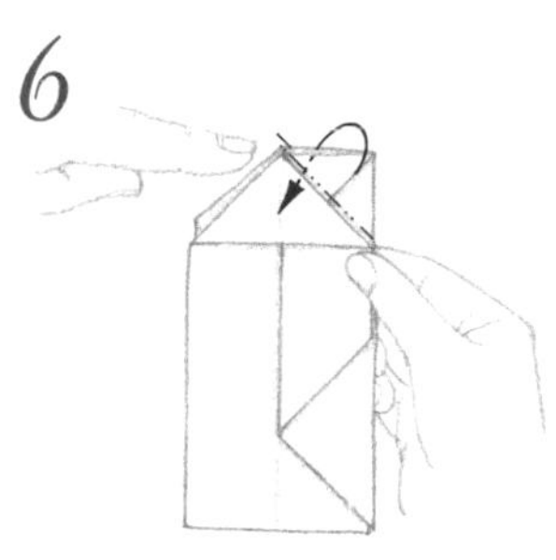

Inside reverse fold the top right-hand corner.

10

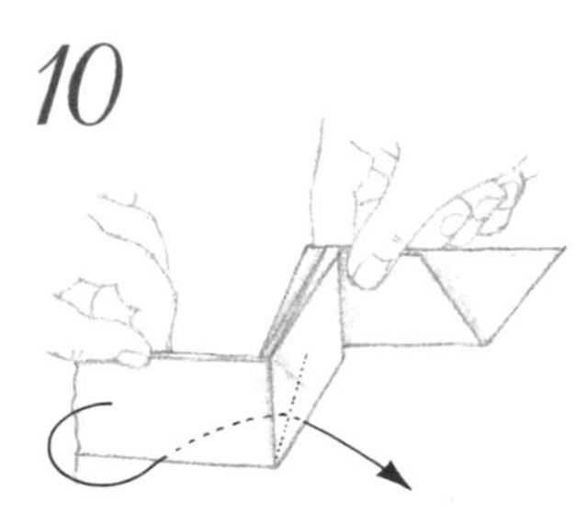

… down as shown.

11

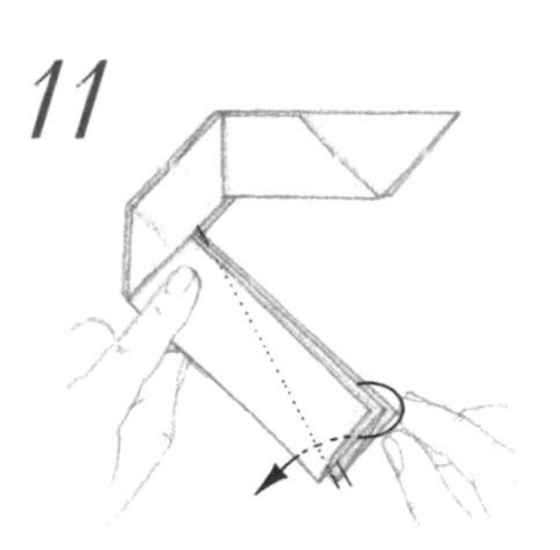

Inside reverse fold the section's middle ridge of paper, to make the snake's head.

12

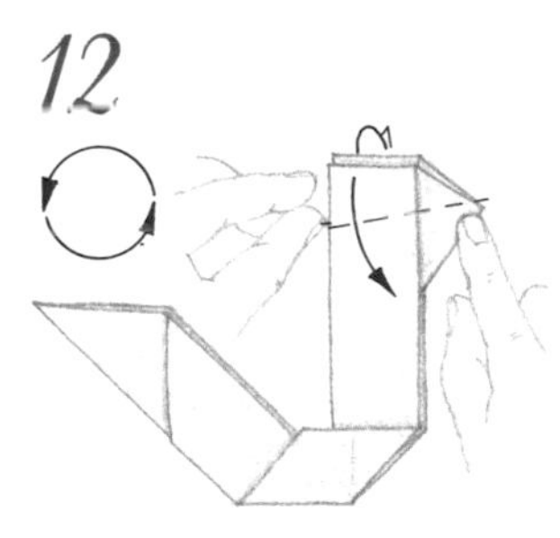

Turn the paper around into the position shown. Valley fold the head's front layer of paper. Repeat behind.

13

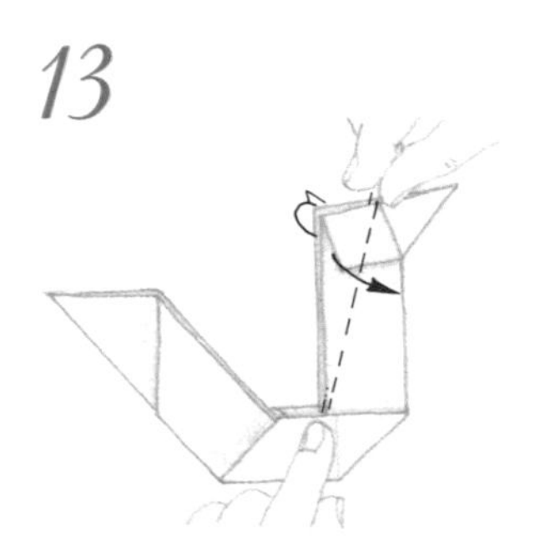

Valley fold the front layer of paper as shown. Repeat behind.

14

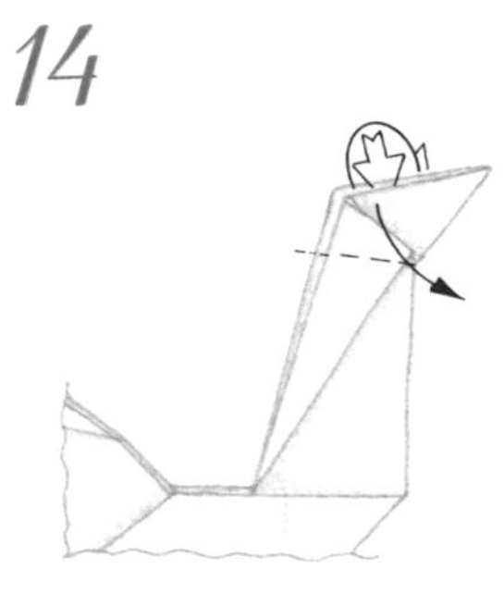

Outside reverse fold the snake's head.

15

Valley fold the head over towards the left a little.

16

17

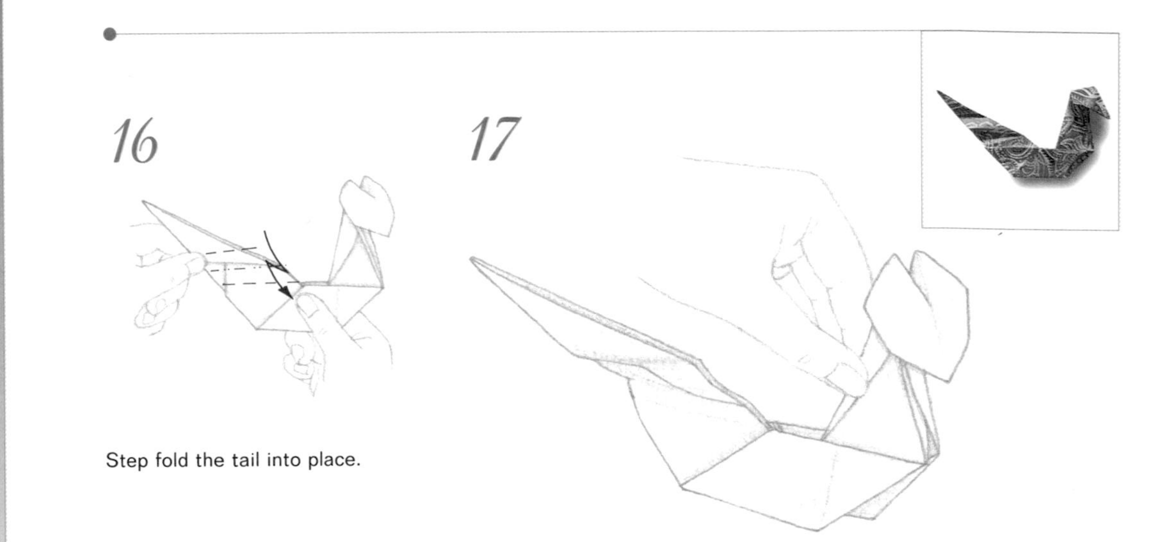

Step fold the tail into place.

Open the base out slightly to complete the snake.

Horse

Making Your Horse

With this model, try to make your cuts and folds as neat and accurate as possible. Use a square piece of paper, white side up. You will also need a pair of scissors.

1

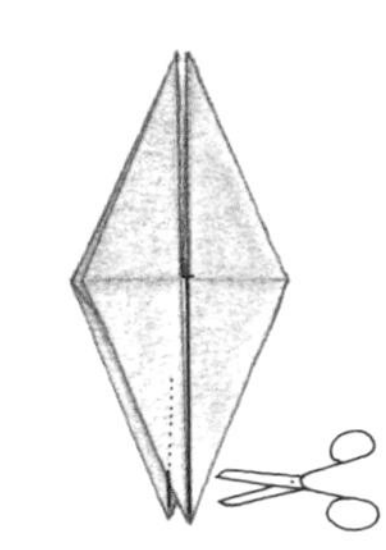

Follow steps 1 to 11 of the crane (*see pages 25–7*). Taking the half that is joined down the middle, cut one layer at a time, being careful not to slit the middle point.

2

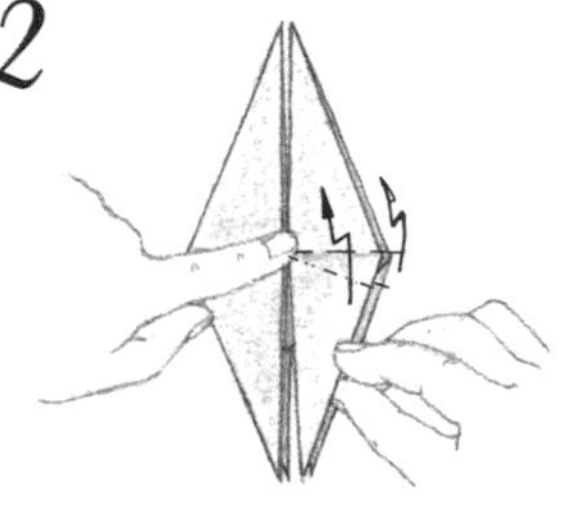

Step fold a lower right-hand flap as shown, to make a back leg. Repeat behind.

3

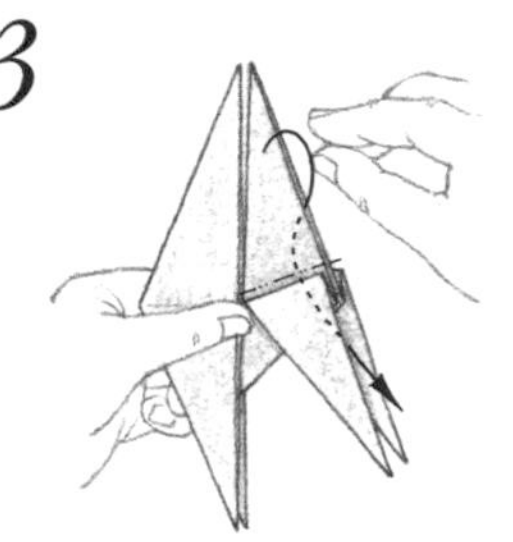

Inside reverse fold the top right-hand point down.

7

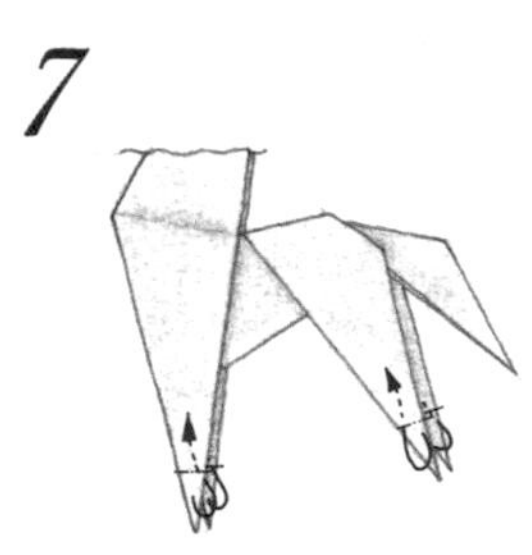

Blunt the horse's legs with inside reverse folds.

8

Inside reverse fold the top point, to make the head.

9

Blunt the snout with an inside reverse fold.

4

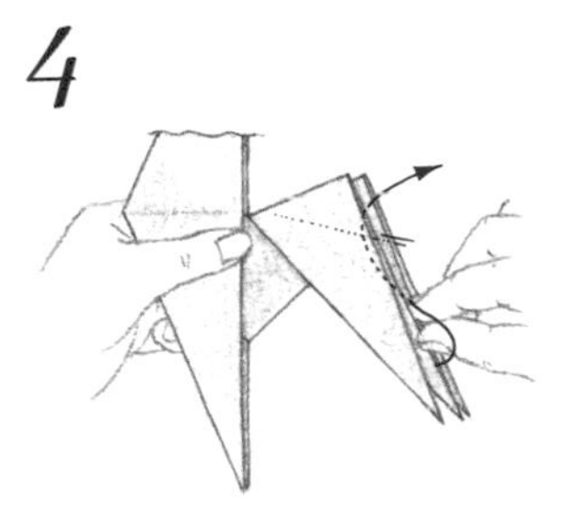

Inside reverse fold the point back up into the position shown in step 5, to make the tail.

5

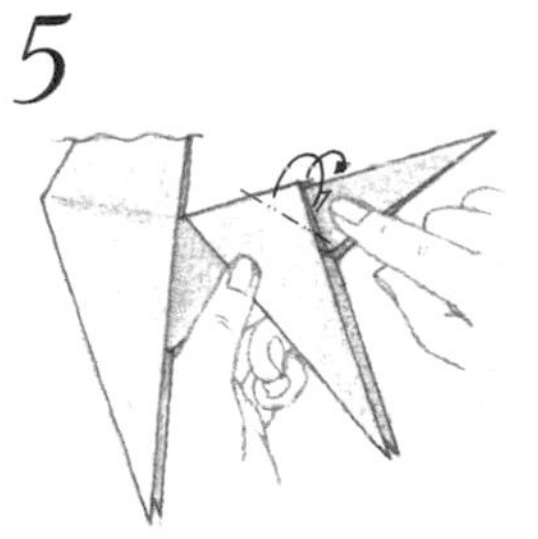

Shape the top of a back leg with a mountain fold. Repeat behind.

6

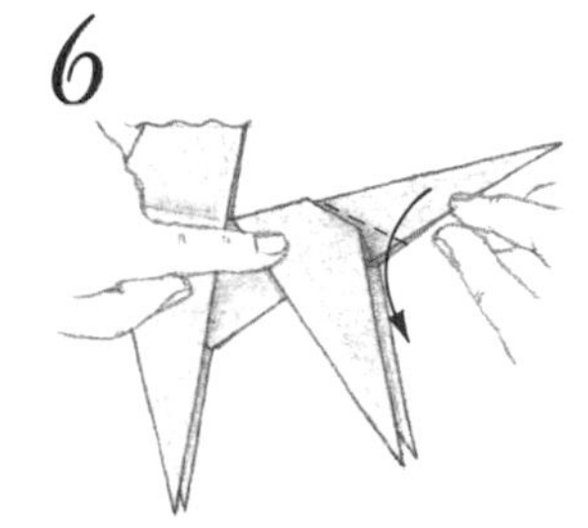

Valley fold the tail as shown.

10

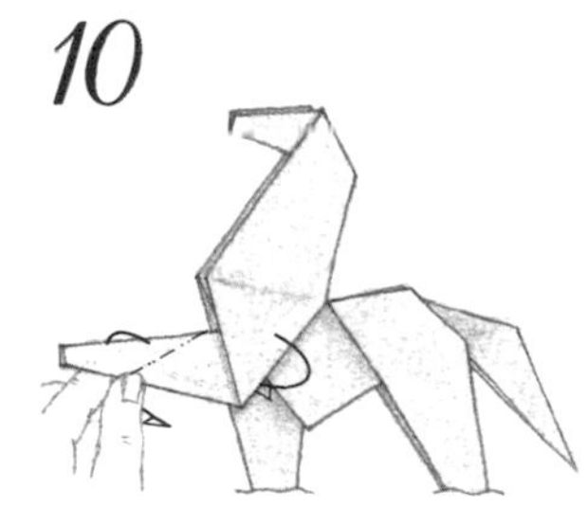

Mountain fold a front leg up, and then down, to suggest movement.

11

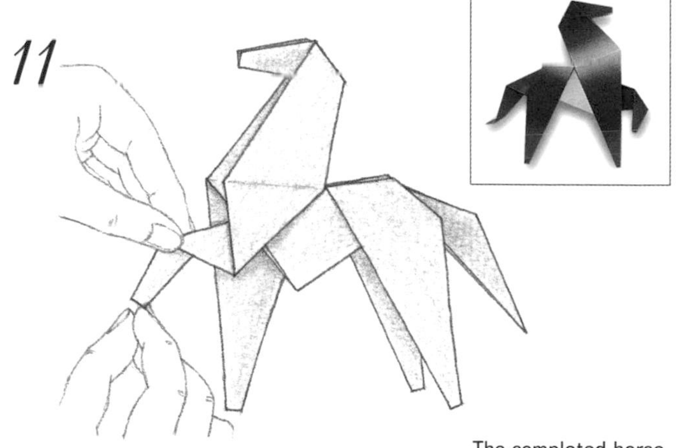

The completed horse.

Phoenix

Making Your Phoenix

This model can at first appear quite difficult. But if you study each illustration carefully to make sure you are following the instructions correctly, making the phoenix will soon become easier. Use a square piece of paper, white side up.

1

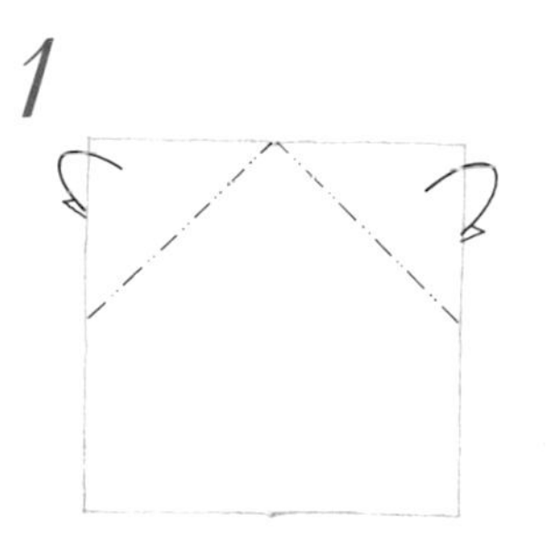

Crease the middle fold-line as shown. Mountain fold the top corners behind to meet the middle fold-line.

2

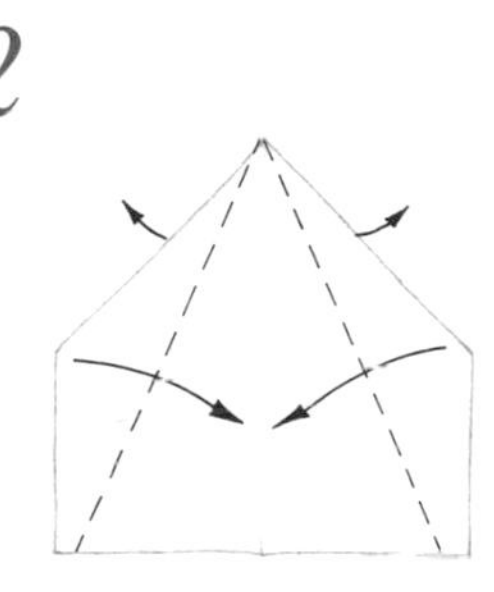

From the top point, valley fold the sloping edges in to meet the middle fold-line, while ...

3

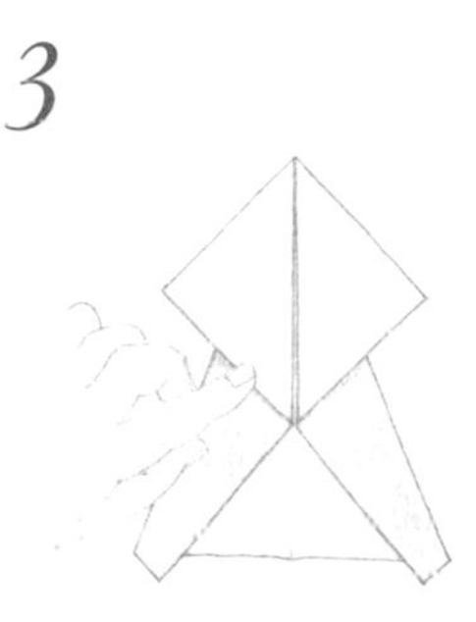

... letting the corners from underneath flick up.

4

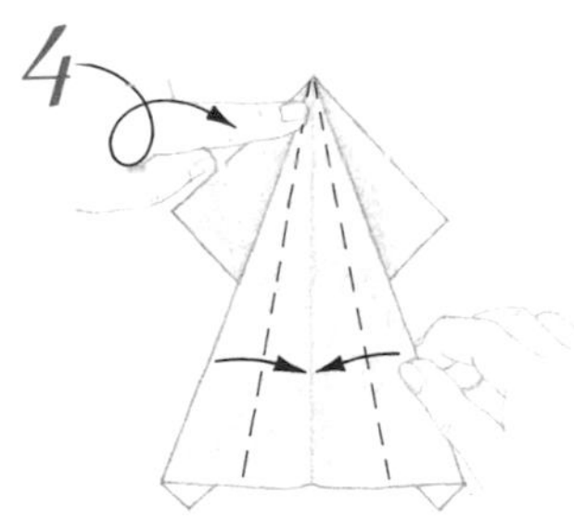

Turn the paper over. From the top point, valley fold the sloping edges in to meet the middle fold-line.

5

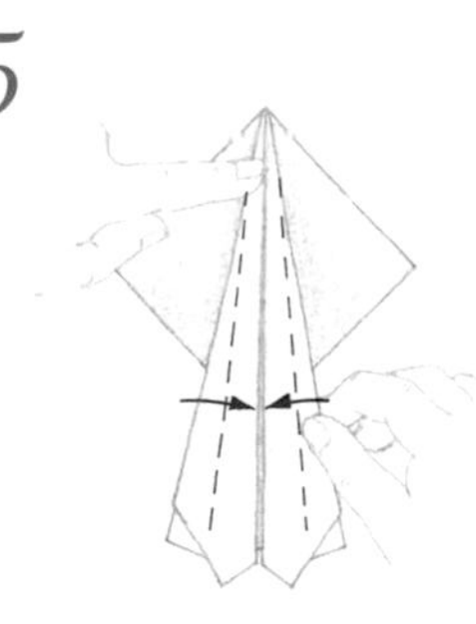

Starting just below the top point, valley fold the sloping edges over towards the middle fold-line.

6

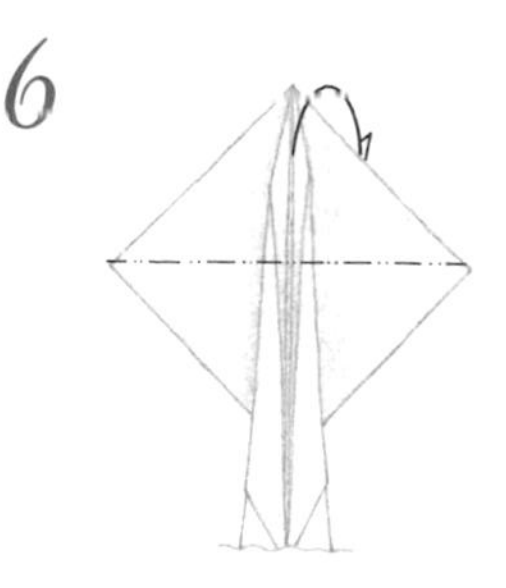

Mountain fold the top point on a line between the two side points.

7

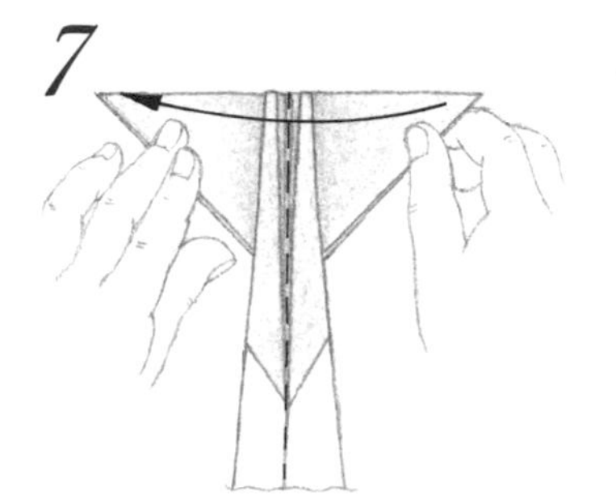

Valley fold the paper in half from right to left.

8

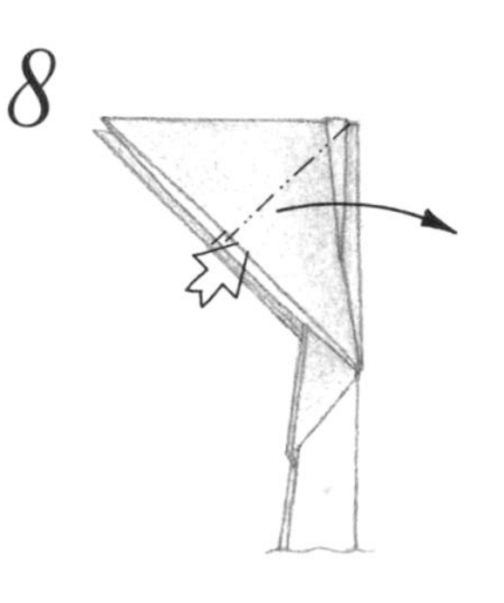

Lift the left-hand point up. Open it out and squash it down neatly into a diamond. Repeat behind, to make a preliminary fold.

9

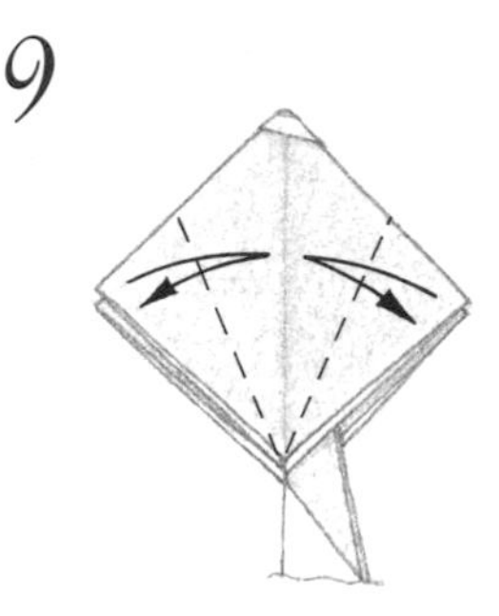

Follow steps 6 to 11 of the crane (*see pages 25–7*) to make a bird base.

13

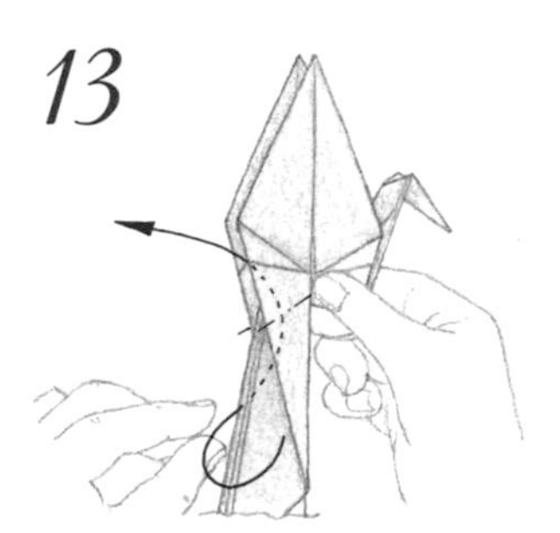

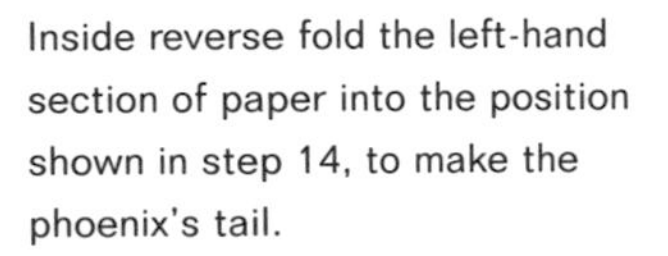

Inside reverse fold the left-hand section of paper into the position shown in step 14, to make the phoenix's tail.

14

Gently pull the wings apart, to flatten the middle point out a little.

15

Open out the tail slightly.

10

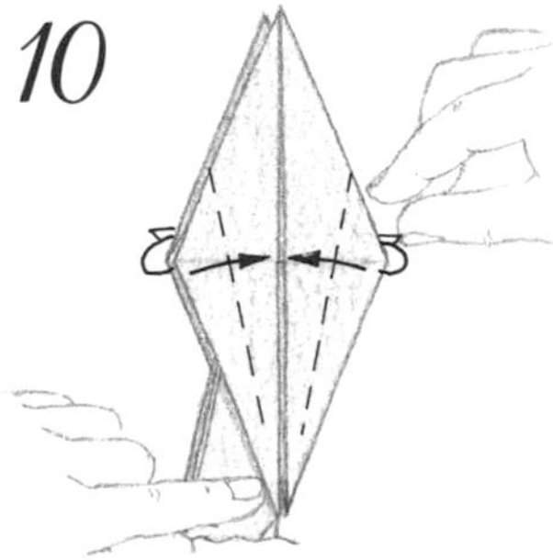

Valley fold the lower sloping edges over, so they lie along the middle line. Repeat behind.

11

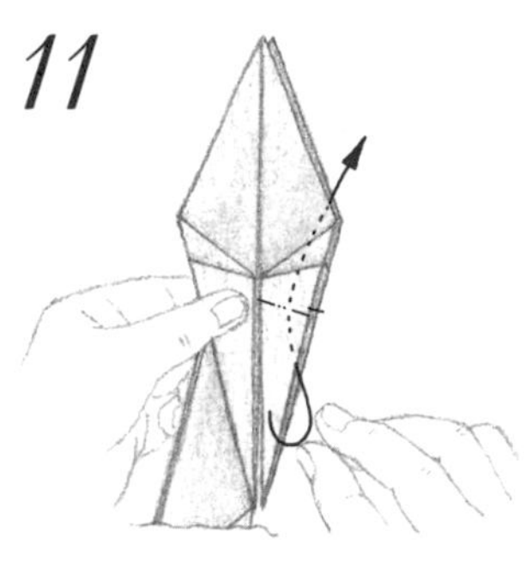

Inside reverse fold the bottom right-hand point into the position shown in step 12.

12

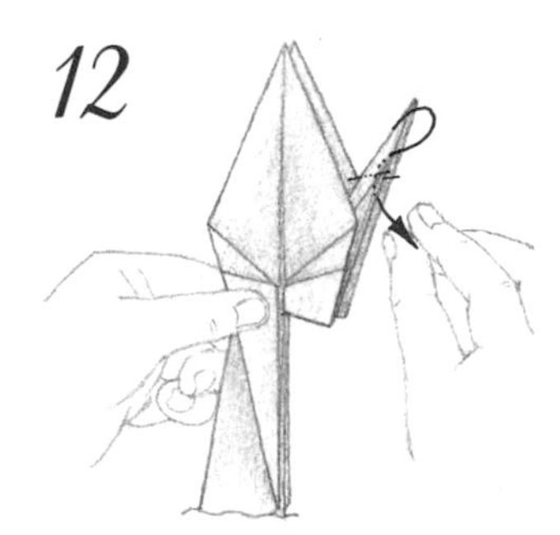

Inside reverse fold the point's tip, to make the head and beak.

16

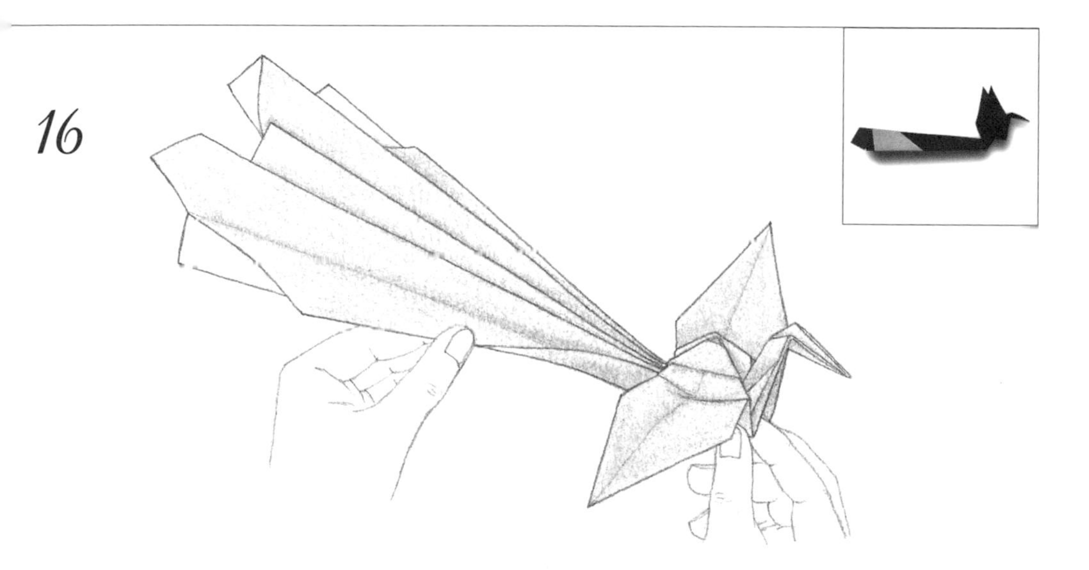

This completes the phoenix.

Tortoise

Making Your Tortoise

The tortoise model is very popular among Japanese children, but is comparatively unknown in the West. Use a square piece of paper, white side up.

1

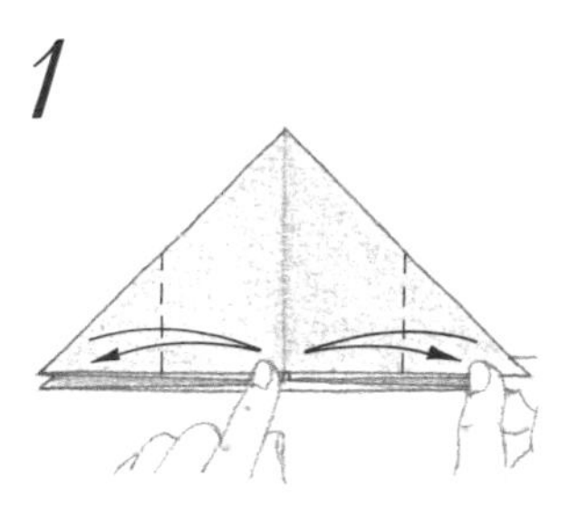

Follow steps 1 to 6 of the goldfish (see page 11) to make a waterbomb base. Fold and unfold the bottom points (top two layers only) as shown.

2

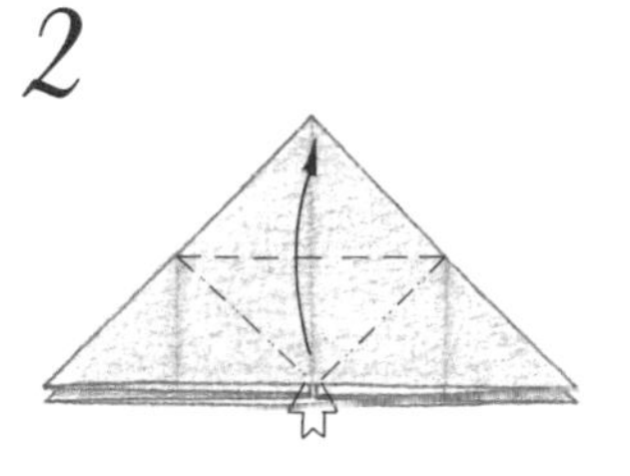

Valley fold the top layer of paper in half from bottom to top …

3

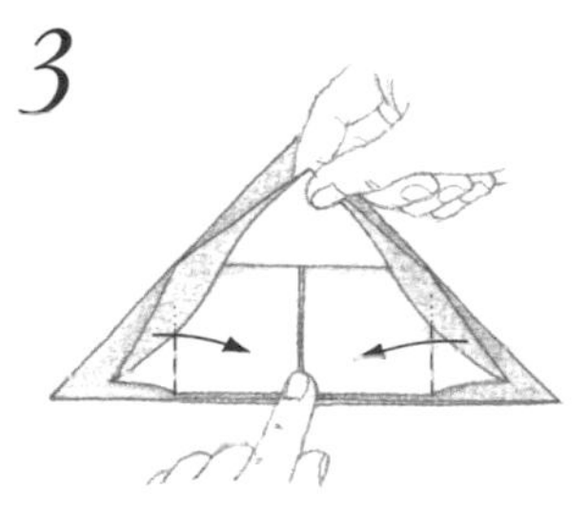

… making the bottom points rise up. Fold the edges in …

4

… so they meet along the middle line.

5

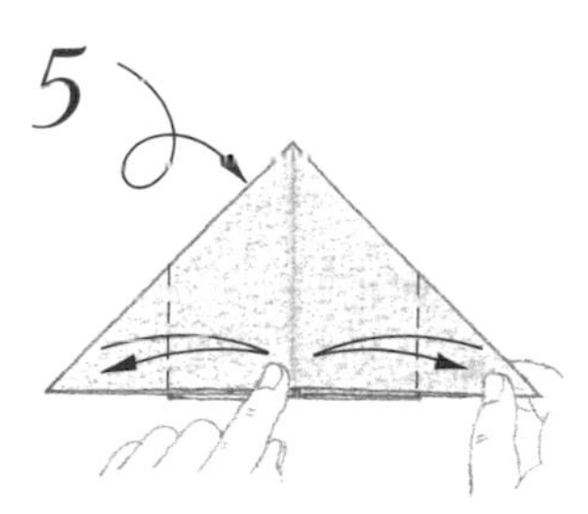

Turn the paper over. Fold and unfold the bottom points as shown. Repeat steps 2 to 4.

6

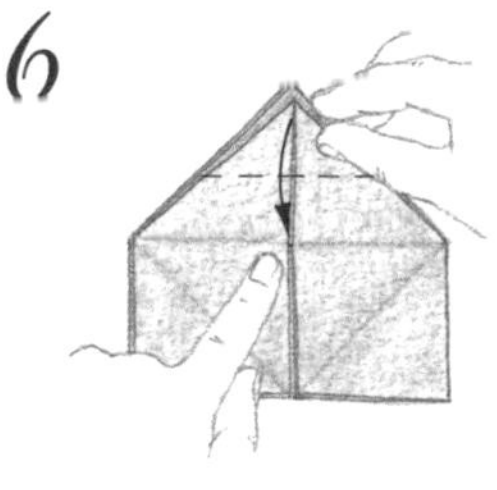

Valley fold the top point in to the middle.

7

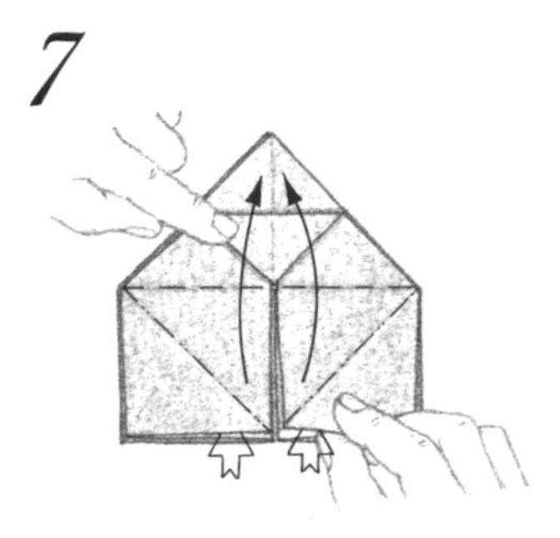

Open up the two square layers at the bottom and ...

8

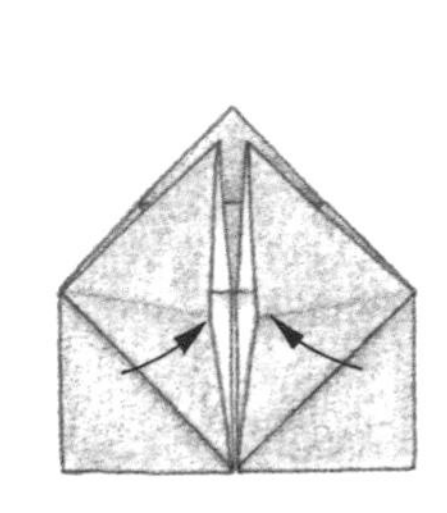

... squash them neatly into triangle shapes.

9

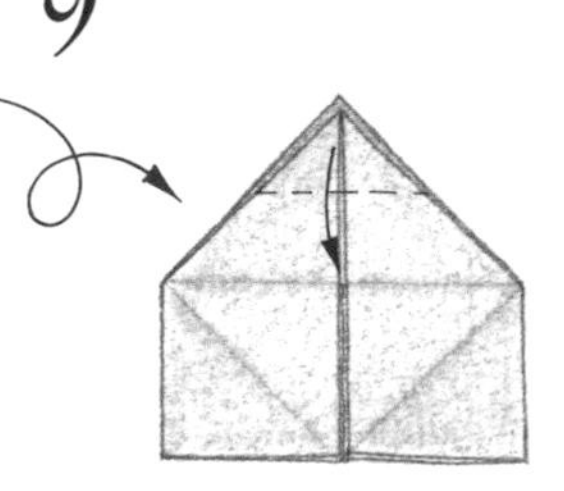

Turn the paper over. Repeat steps 6 to 8.

13

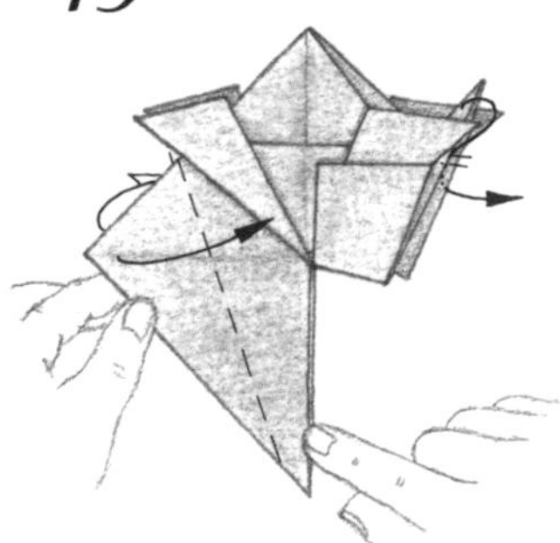

Inside reverse fold the point's tip, to make the tail. Valley fold the left-hand sloping edge, as shown. Repeat behind.

14

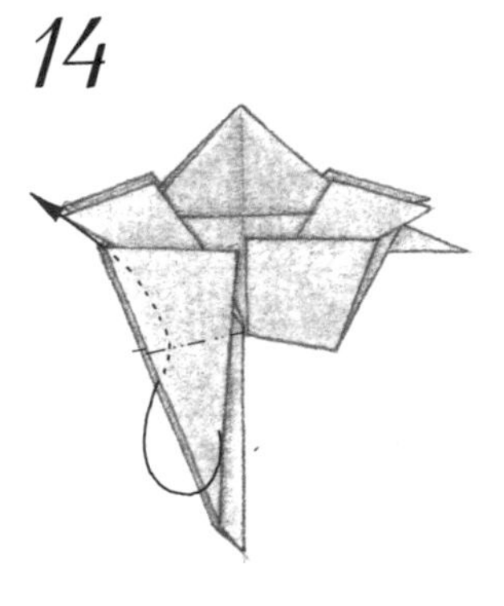

Inside reverse fold the bottom left-hand point, to make the tortoise's neck.

15

Gently pull the legs apart while flattening out the middle point a little, so the tortoise becomes three-dimensional.

10

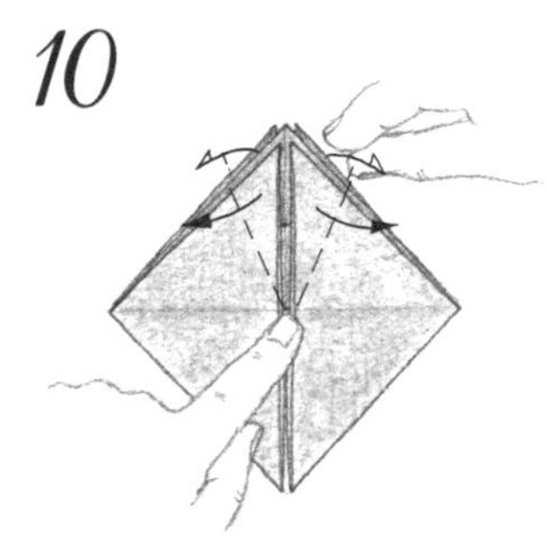

Valley fold the top points out from the middle, as shown, to make two of the legs. Repeat behind.

11

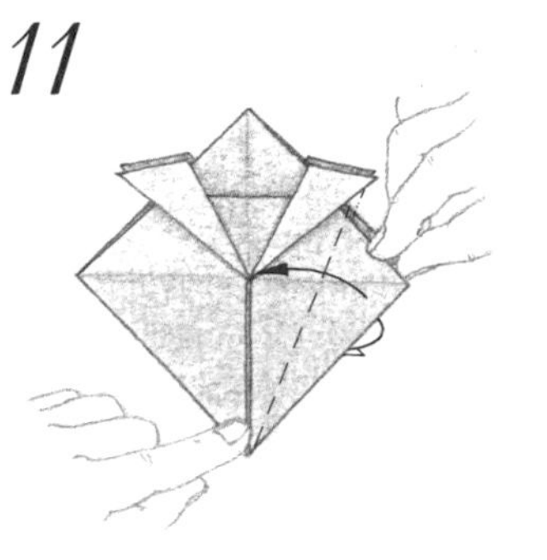

From the bottom point, valley fold the right-hand sloping edge over, so that it lies along the middle line. Repeat behind.

12

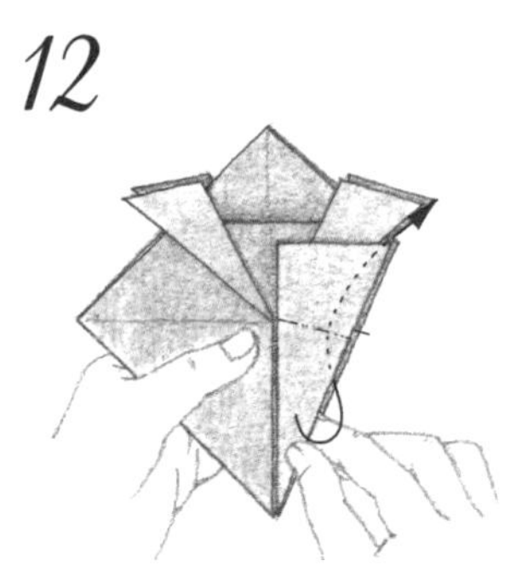

Inside reverse fold the bottom right-hand point.

16

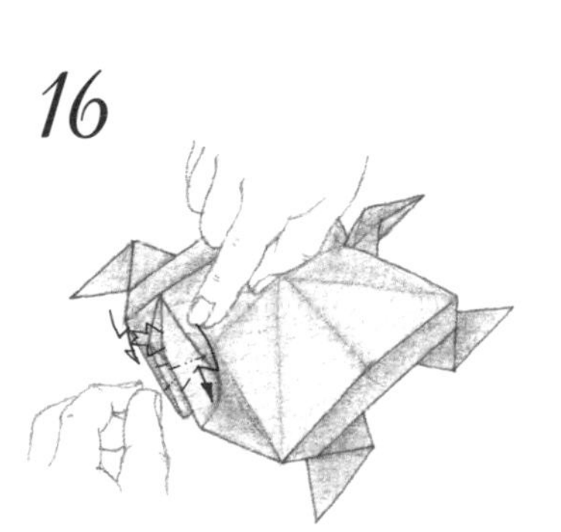

Step fold the neck on either side, as shown, to make the tortoise's head.

17

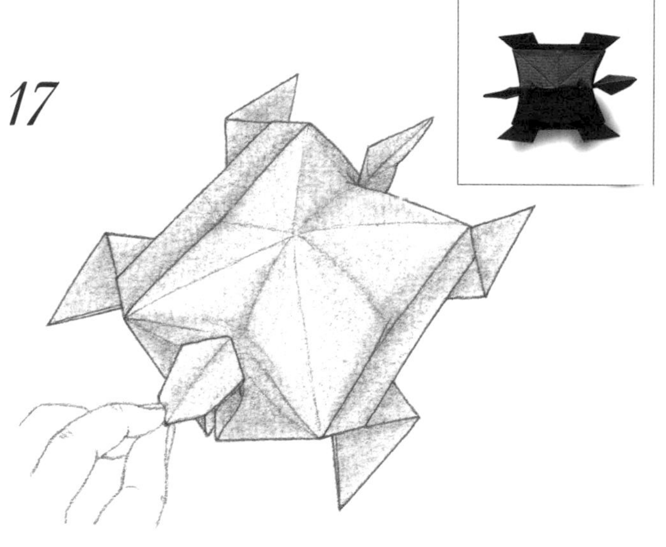

The completed tortoise.

Tiger

Making Your Tiger

The procedure involving two pieces of origami that are joined together to make one model is called compound origami. This technique is very useful for making animals. Use two squares of paper equal in size. You will also need a pair of scissors and some glue.

1

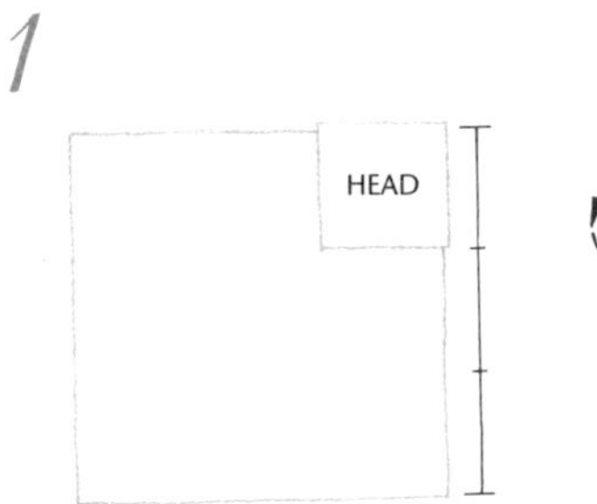

Cut one piece to the size shown and set aside. Fold the other into a bird base, following steps 1 to 11 of the crane (*see pages 25–7*).

2

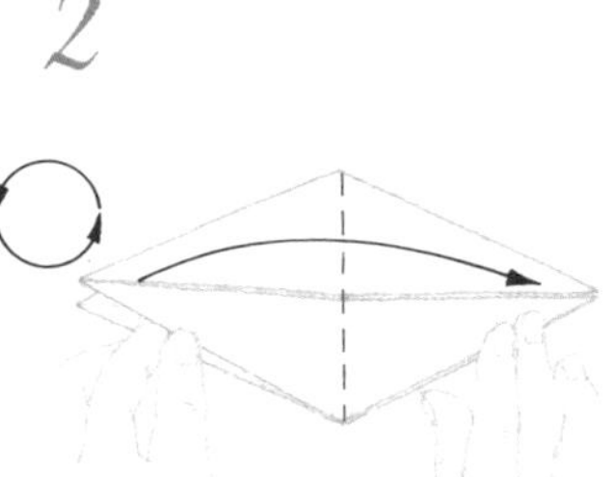

To make the body: Turn the bird base so the half that is joined down the middle points left. Valley fold the top flap from left to right.

3

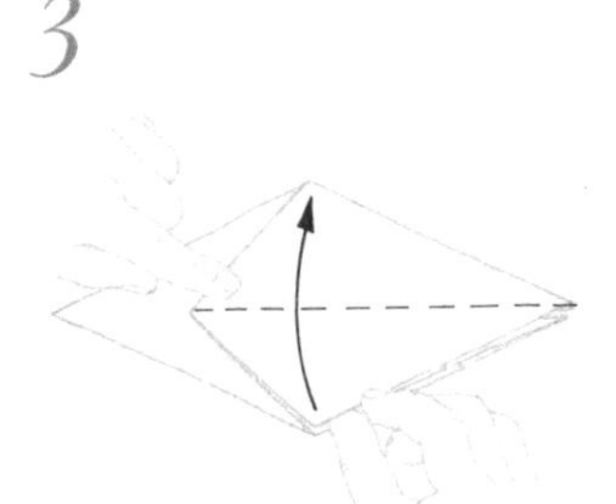

Valley fold the bottom point up (top layer only).

4

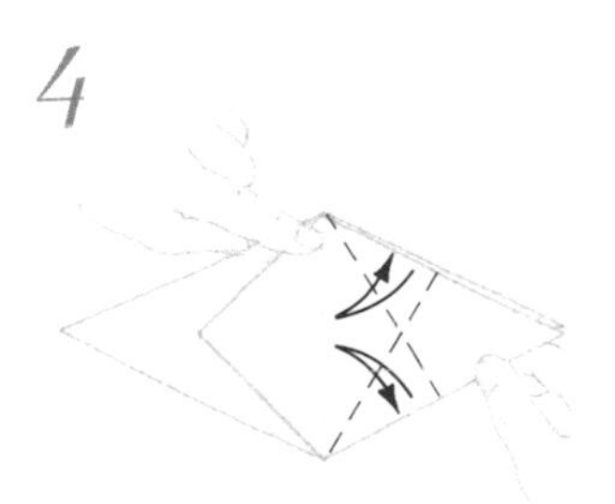

Fold and unfold the top right-hand flap as shown.

5

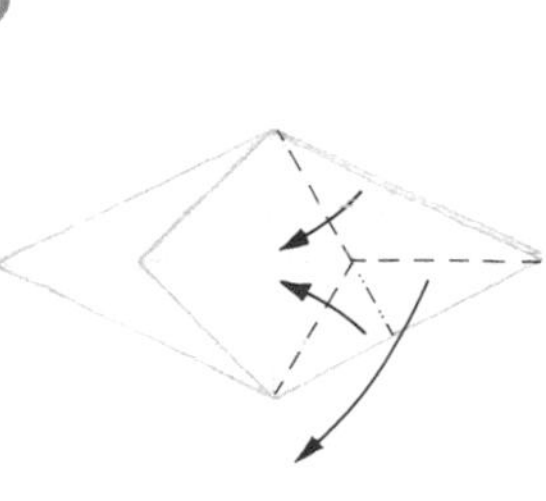

Pinch the flap's sloping edges together along the existing fold-lines, to make a point, as shown.

6

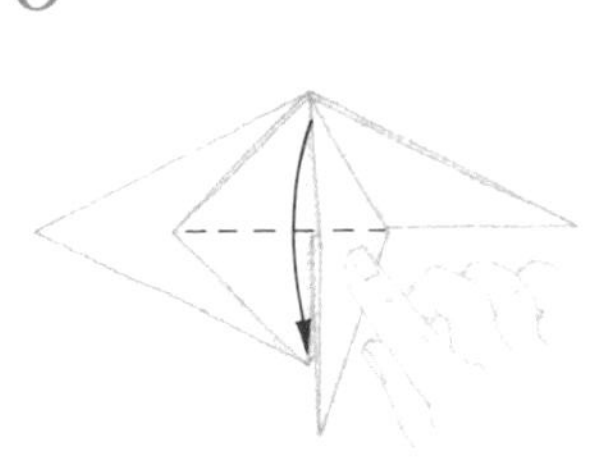

Flatten the point downwards. Take the point at the top, and valley fold the upper two layers down.

7

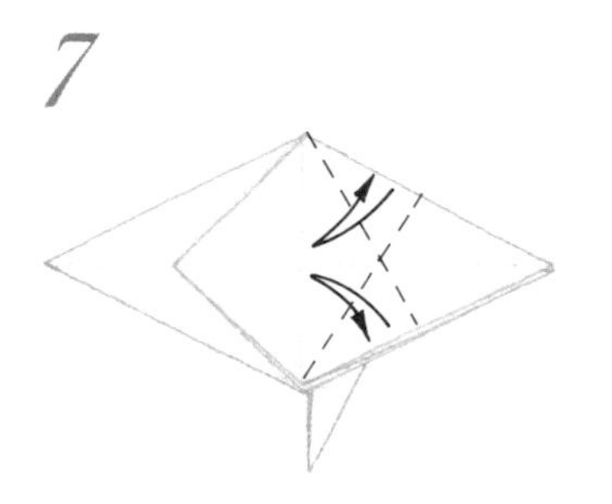

Repeat steps 4 and 5, but this time ...

8

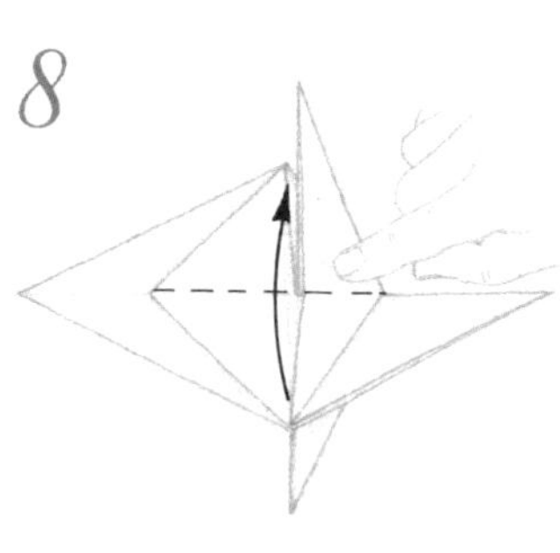

... flatten the point upwards. Valley fold the bottom point up (top layer only).

9

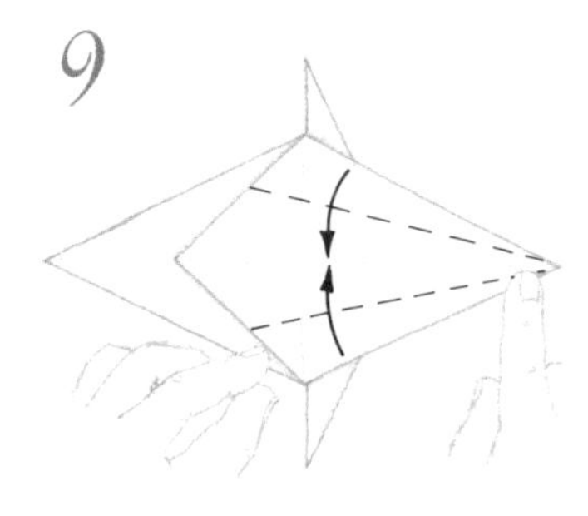

From the right-hand point, valley fold the sloping edges in to meet the middle fold-line.

13

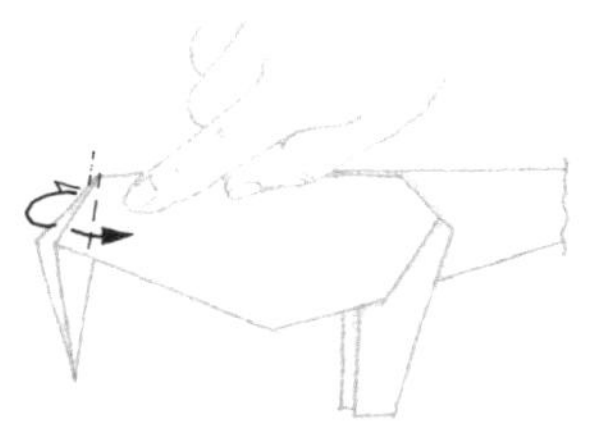

Valley fold the reversed point towards the right, as shown. Repeat behind, to make the front legs.

14

Blunt the front legs with an inside reverse fold. Give the right-hand point one or two inside reverse folds to create the tail. This completes the body.

15

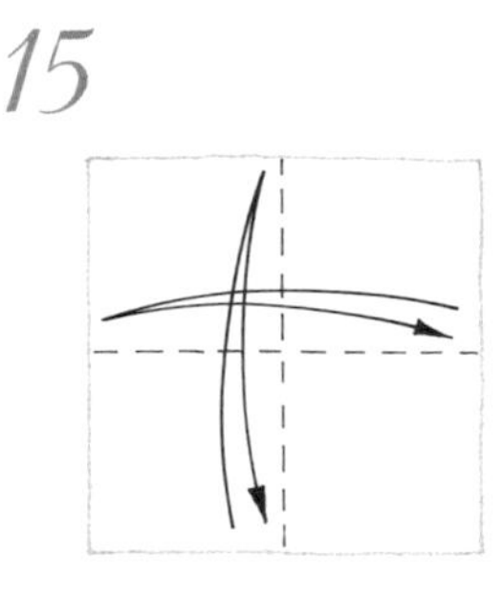

To make the head: Take the smaller square that you prepared in step 1 and crease the middle fold-lines as shown.

10

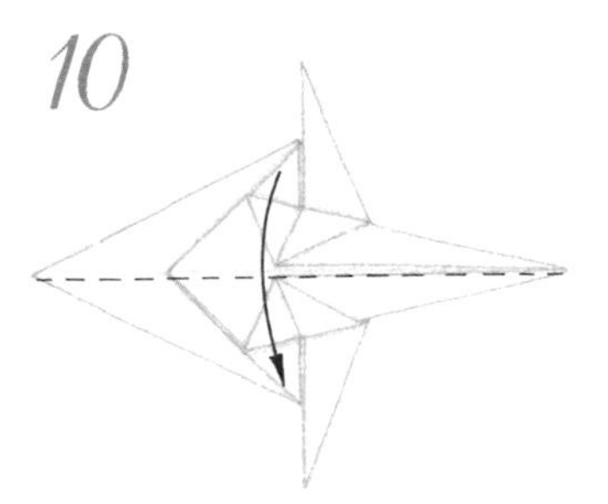

Valley fold the whole model in half from top to bottom. There should now be two triangles pointing downwards

11

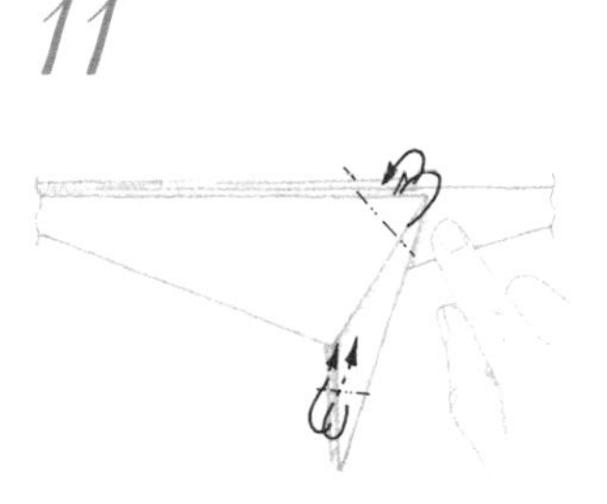

Blunt the tips of these triangles with an inside reverse fold, to make the back legs. Mountain fold the tops of the back legs to shape them.

12

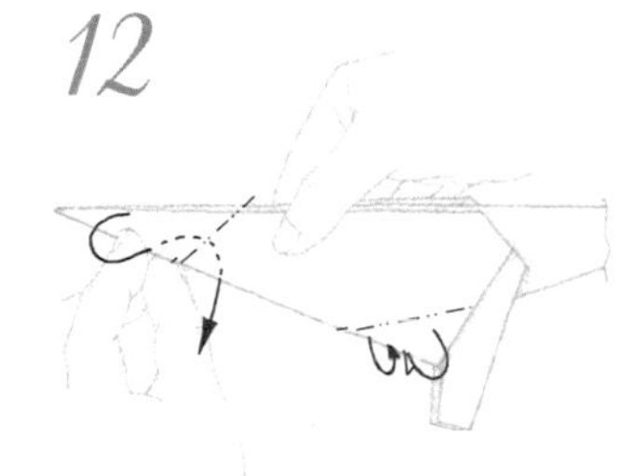

Inside reverse fold the left hand point. Shape the tiger's underside with a mountain fold. Repeat behind.

16

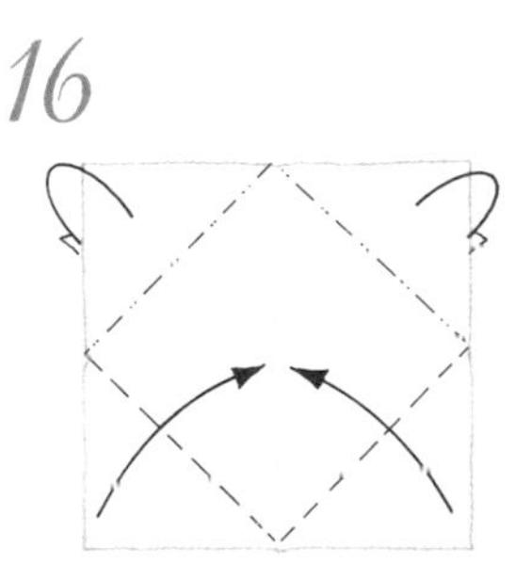

Mountain fold the top corners, and valley fold the bottom corners, in to the middle.

17

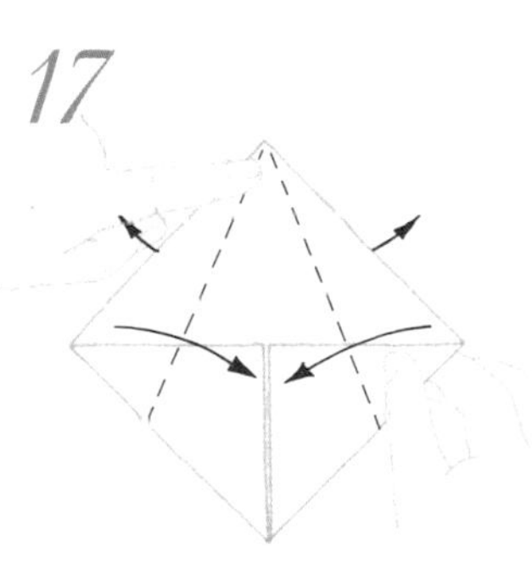

From the top point, valley fold the sloping edges in to meet the middle fold-line, while letting the corners from underneath flick up.

18

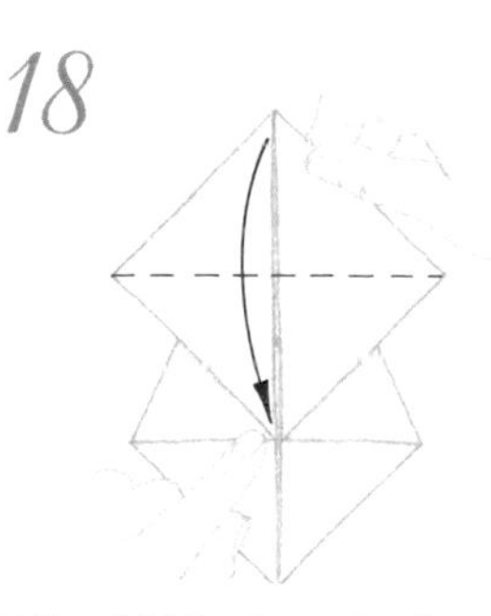

Valley fold the top point down on a line between the two side points.

19

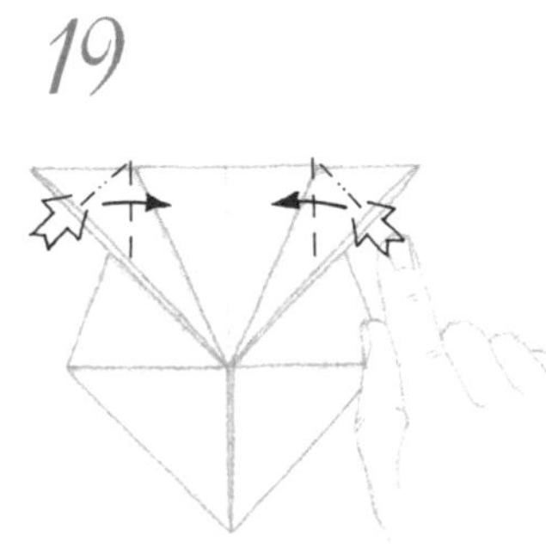

Open out each side point and squash them down neatly into diamonds.

20

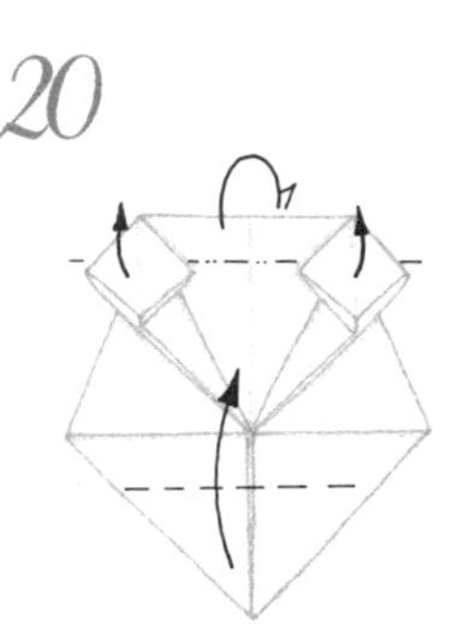

Mountain fold the top edge while folding back the top layer of each diamond, to make the ears. Valley fold the bottom flap up …

21

… and fold its tip over and over to make the nose. To complete the head, shape its sides with mountain folds.

22

23

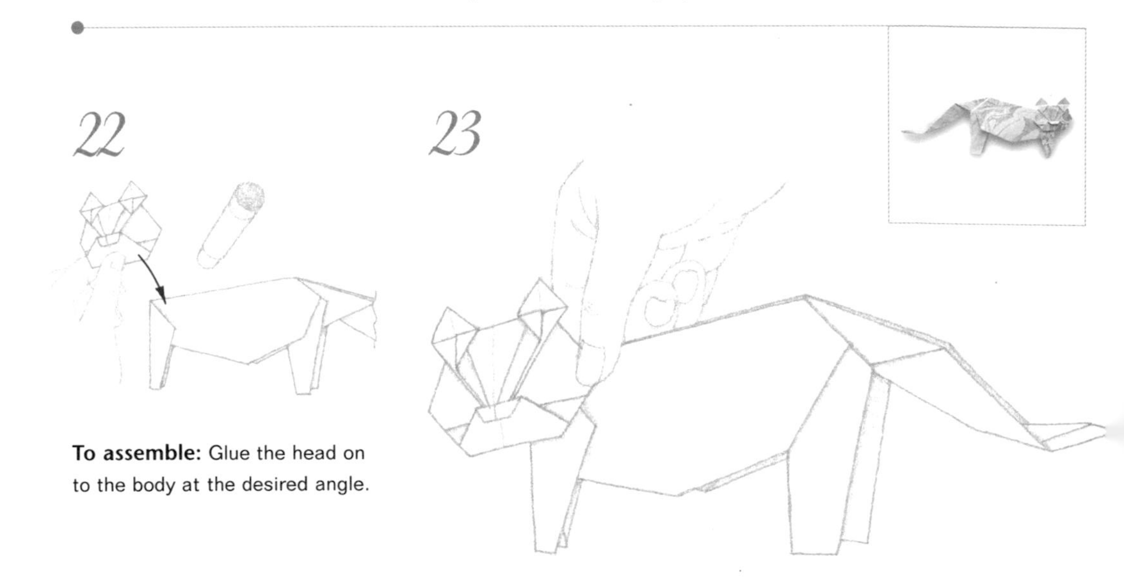

To assemble: Glue the head on to the body at the desired angle.

Your finished tiger.

Dragon

Making Your Dragon

This compound origami model is made up of two similar units, so be very careful not to mix up your paper or the folding steps. Use two squares of paper equal in size. You will also need some glue.

1

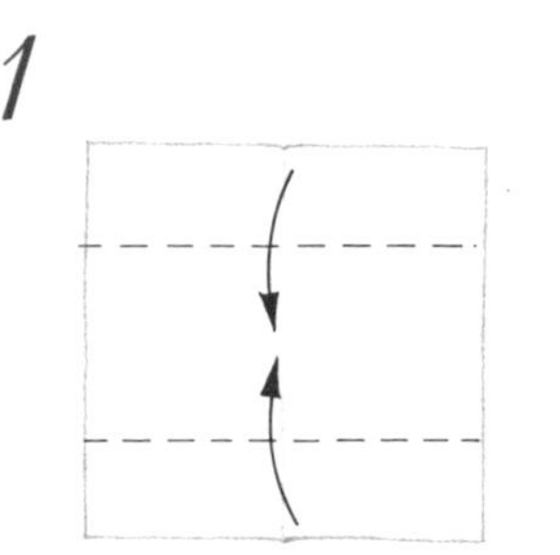

To make the front half: Taking one square white side up, crease the middle fold-line. Valley fold the top and bottom edges to meet it.

2

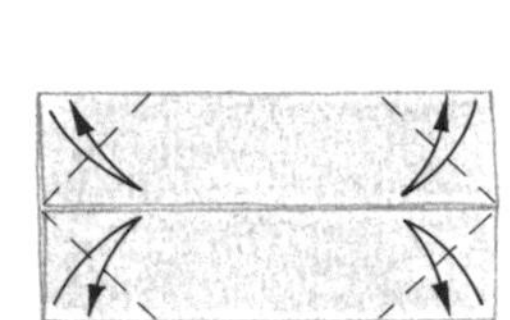

Fold and unfold the right- and left-hand corners as shown.

3

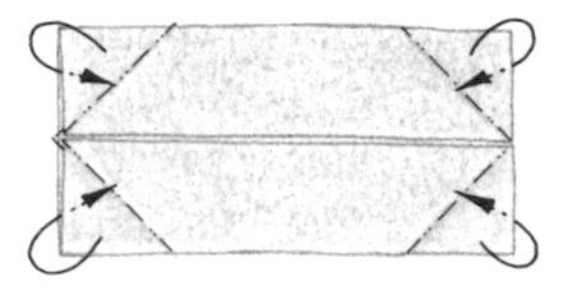

Inside reverse fold the corners along the fold-lines made in step 2.

7

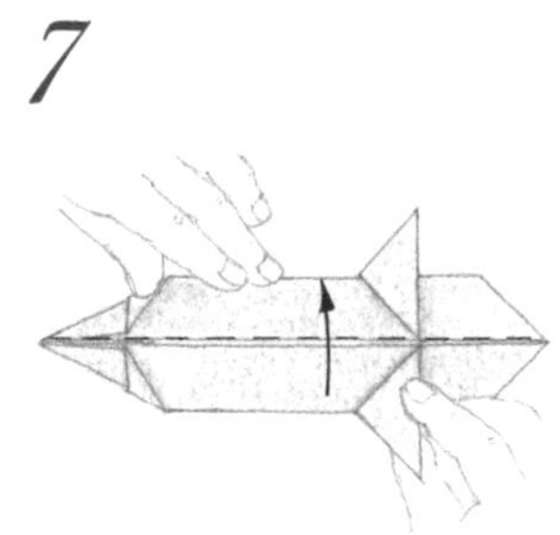

Valley fold the paper in half from bottom to top.

8

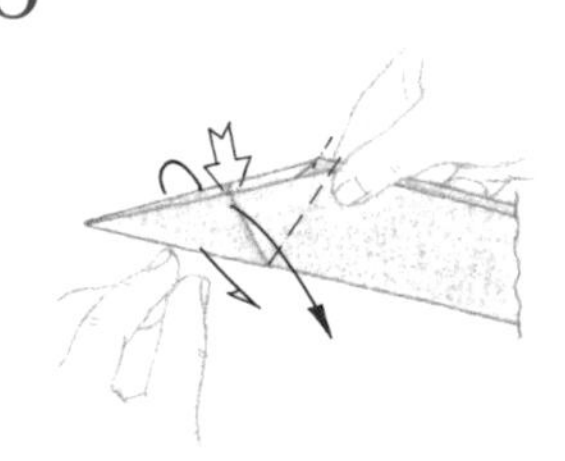

Outside reverse fold the left-hand point, to make the dragon's head.

9

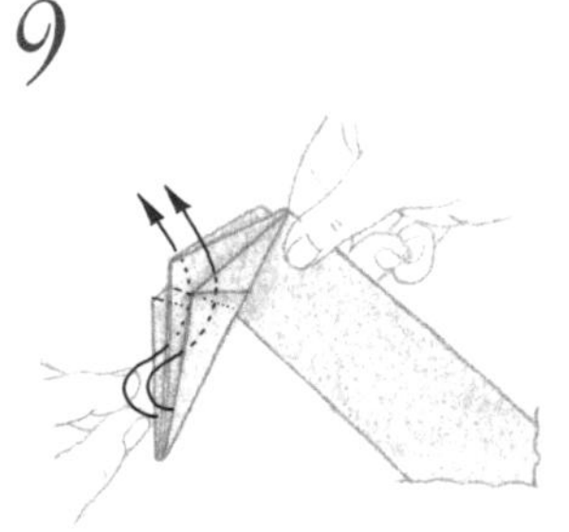

Inside reverse fold the two points that are hidden inside the front of the head, to make the dragon's horns.

4

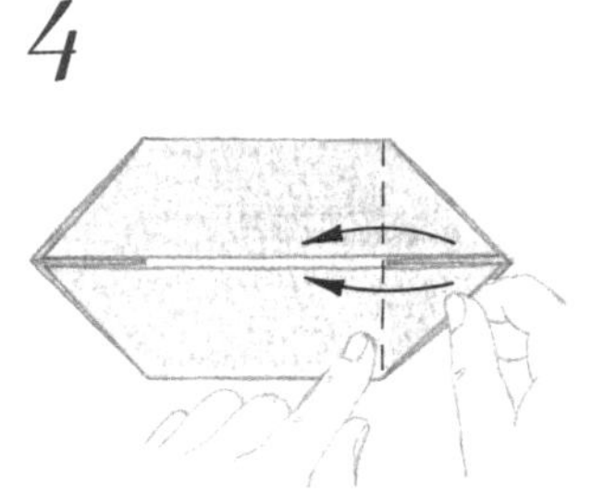

Valley fold the right-hand points (top layer only) over to the left.

5

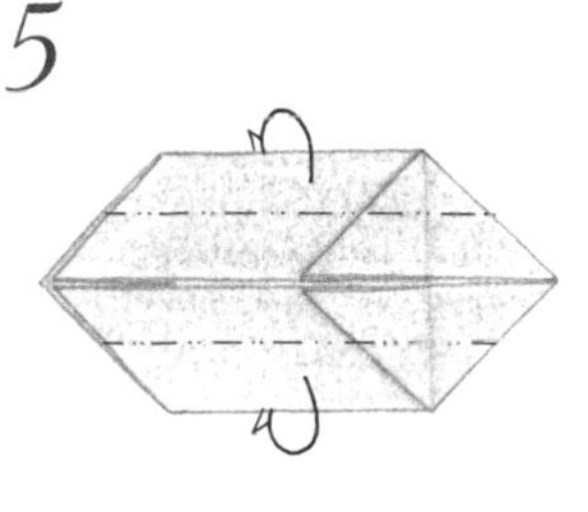

Mountain fold the top and bottom edges behind to meet the middle fold-line.

6

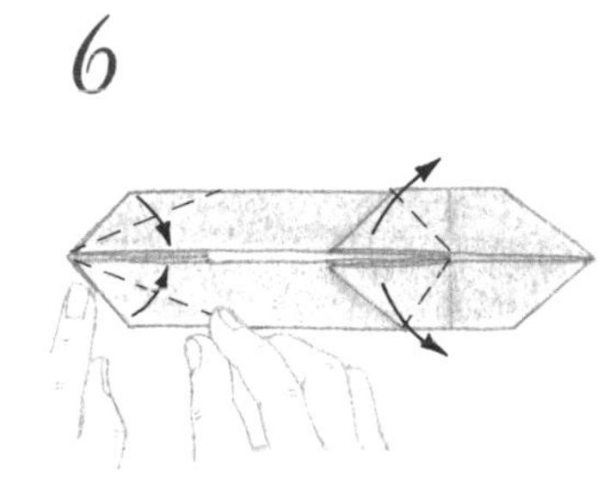

From the left-hand point, valley fold the corners in to the middle fold-line. Valley fold the right-hand points outwards as shown.

10

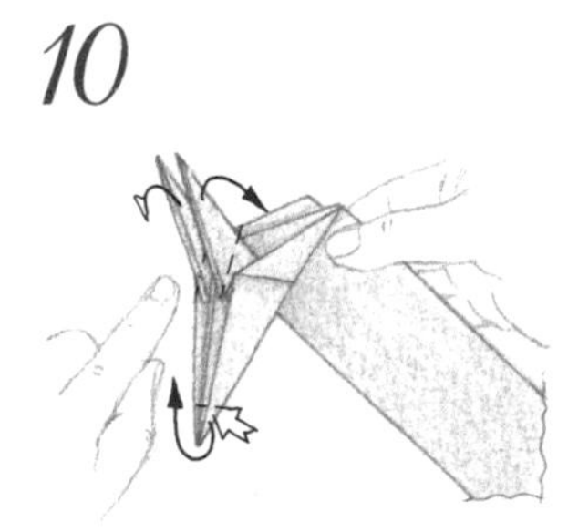

Valley fold the horns out to either side. Shape the snout with an outside reverse fold.

11

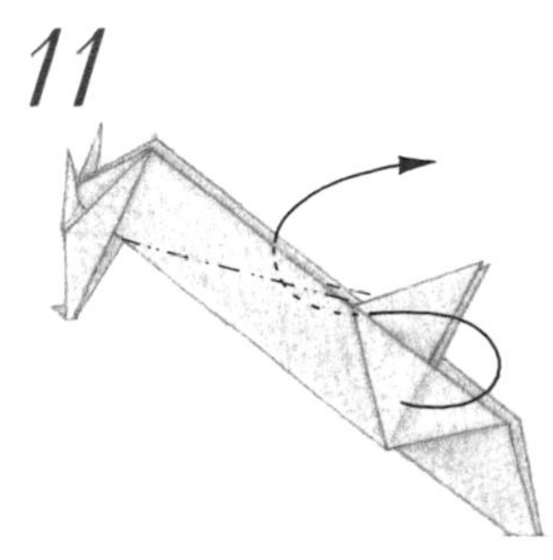

Inside reverse fold the lower section of paper up to the right.

12

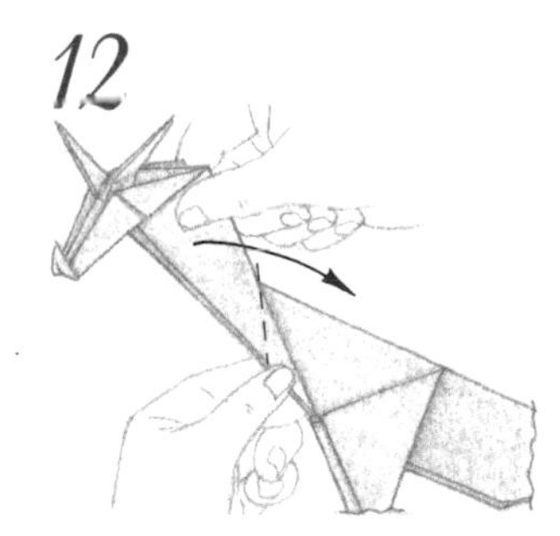

To complete the front half of your dragon, valley fold the head over towards the right.

13

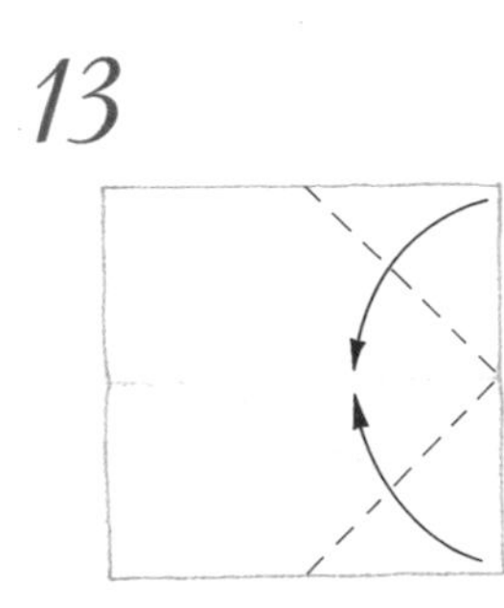

To make the back half: Taking the second square white side up, crease the middle fold-line. Valley fold the right-hand corners.

14

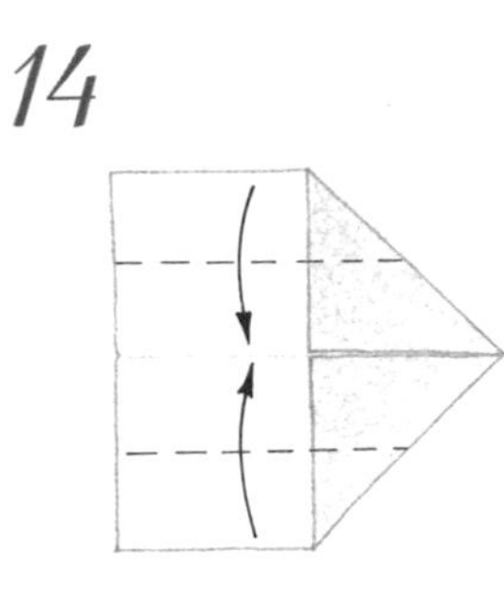

Valley fold the top and bottom edges in to meet the middle fold-line.

15

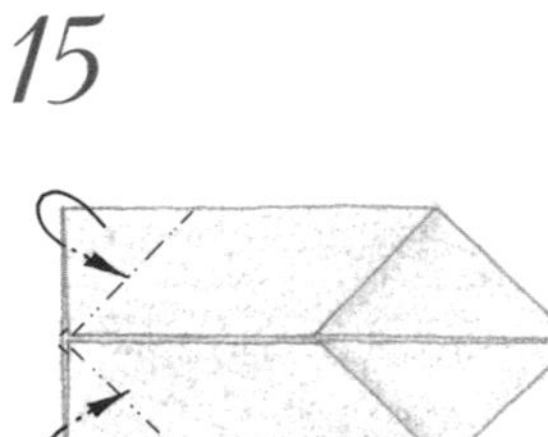

Inside reverse fold the left-hand corners.

19

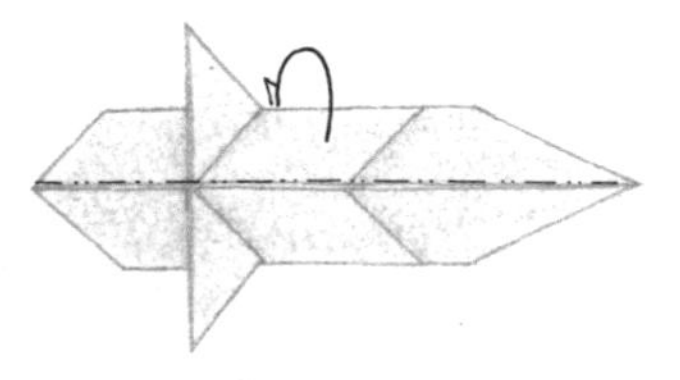

Mountain fold the paper in half from top to bottom.

20

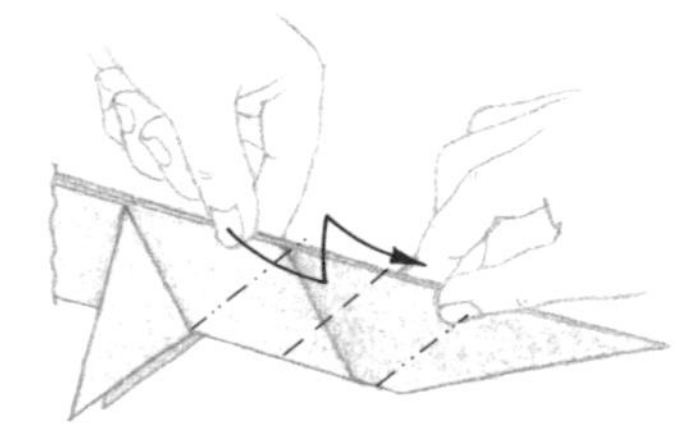

Step fold the right-hand point as shown ...

21

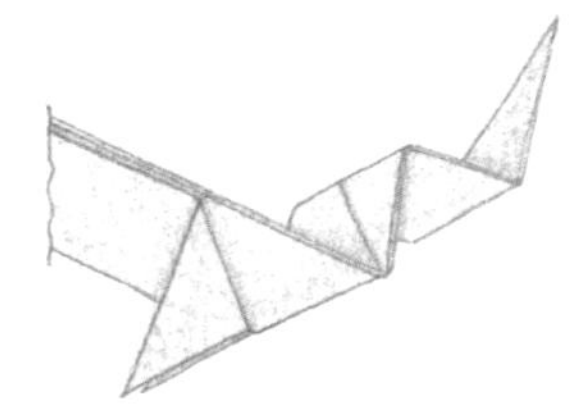

... to complete the tail.

16

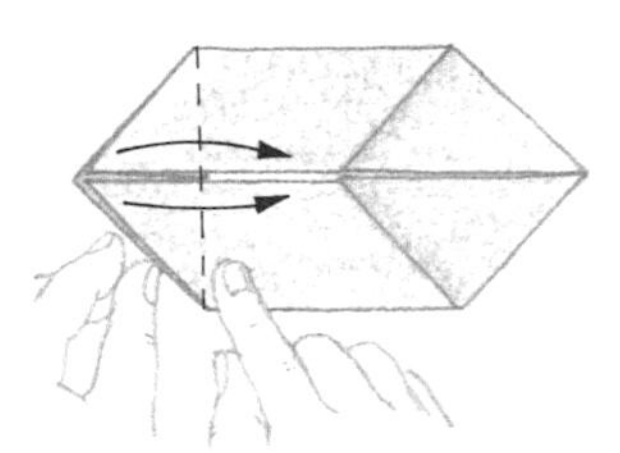

Valley fold the left-hand points (top layer only) over to the right.

17

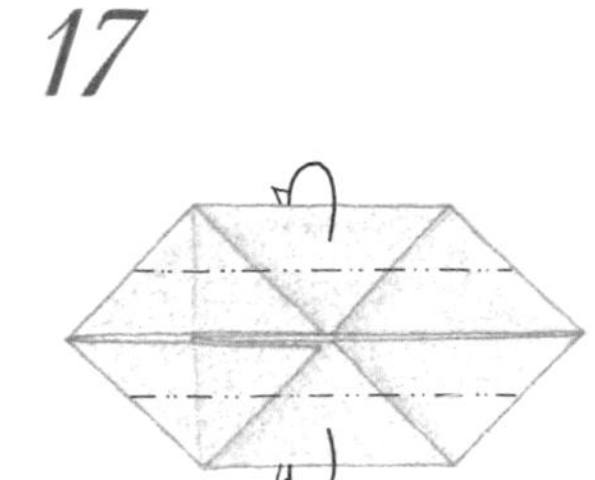

Mountain fold the top and bottom edges behind to meet the middle fold-line.

18

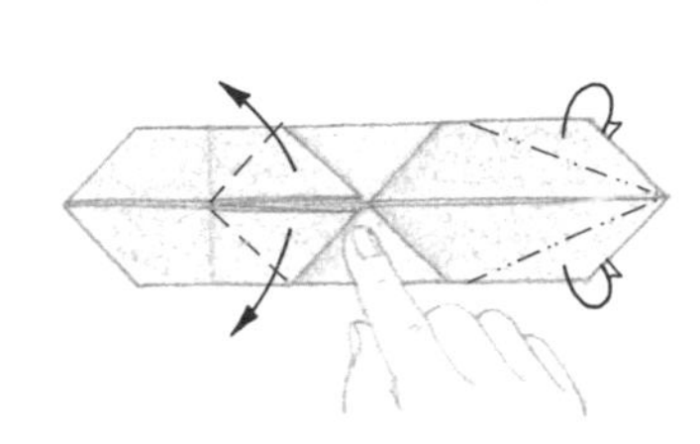

From the right hand point, mountain fold the corners to meet the middle fold-line. Valley fold the two pointed flaps outwards.

22

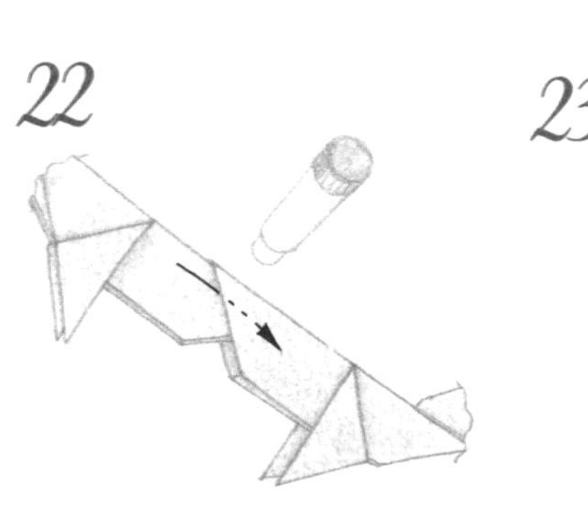

To assemble: Tuck the front section inside the back section as shown. Glue them together.

23

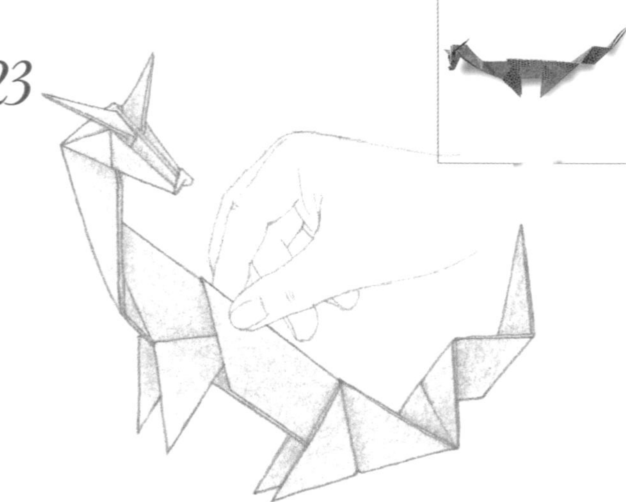

The completed dragon.

Useful Addresses

The increasing popularity and international interest in origami is evident today in the number of organizations around the world that are devoted to it. Most paper-folding societies publish a newsletter or magazine containing origami-related articles and illustrations for new folds. They also hold regular meetings and yearly conventions that may include practical classes and exhibitions of the latest creations. They welcome folding enthusiasts of any age or level.

Origami

The following organizations offer a broad range of origami books, private publications on the various aspects of paper folding, packaged origami paper, and information on the many international origami associations.

The Membership Secretary,
British Origami Society
2a The Chestnuts, Countesthorpe,
Leicestershire LE8 5TL, England
www.britishorigami.org.uk

O.U.S.A. Center of America
15 West 77th Street, New York,
New York 10024-5192, USA
www.origami-usa.org

Visit Joseph Wu's origami website at: www.origami.vancouver.bc.ca

Japan Origami Academic Society
1-33-8-216 Hakusan,
Bunkyo-ku 113-0001, Tokyo, Japan
www.origami.gr.jp

The Nippon Origami Association
2-064 Domir Gobancho,
12 Gobancho, Chiyoda-ku,
Tokyo 102-0076, Japan
www.origami-noa.com

The Australian Origami Society
www.freewebs.com/perthorigami

Further Reading

Biddle, Steve and Megumi, *Origami Inspired By Japanese Prints*, British Museum Press, in association with The Metropolitan Museum of Art, New York 1998

Kenneway, Eric, *Complete Origami*, Ebury Press, London 1987

Harbin, Robert, *Teach Yourself Origami*, Hodder & Stoughton Ltd, London 2003

Resources

You can purchase additional origami paper from Asian gift shops and toy stores, and also art and craft suppliers and stationers, some of which also stock textured and decorated paper. For beautifully patterned models, try using gift wrap, or to make them even more unusual, experiment with opalescent papers or paper-backed metallic foil. All kinds of paper can be used for origami – writing paper, typing paper, computer paper, and even pages cut from magazines.

Acknowledgements

We would like to thank: John Cunliffe for his assistance with writing The Origins of Origami section of this book; for sharing their original origami designs, our friends in the Nippon Origami Association: Toshio Chino, Takenao Handa, Kunihiko Kasahara, Taiko Niwa, Yasuhiro Sano, Tomoko Tanaka and the estate of Toshie Takahama; for reviewing the text, Ben Brooks, Rachael Brown and Shenna Tilley. A special thank you to Ian and Donna Carter and their family for testing the folding instructions. Credit and thanks for their creative assistance to Takeshi Morikawa and his daughter Aiko. Finally, we would like to express our gratitude to the staff at Eddison Sadd Editions.

EDDISON • SADD EDITIONS
Editorial Director....Ian Jackson
Managing Editor....Tessa Monina
Editor....Katie Ginn
Proofreader....Peter Kirkham
Art Director....Elaine Partington
Designer....Zoe Mellors
Mac Designer....Brazzle Atkins
Production....Carol Anne Herron, Nick Eddison

馬龍紙馬龍紙

花折花折

馬龍紙龍紙馬

花折折花

馬龍紙馬龍紙

花折花折